PRAISE FOR *FERTILE IMAGINATION*

"Melissa is an inspiring display of tenacity and motivation. Whenever you're feeling stuck, peruse Melissa's thoughtfully compiled tips and exercises and you'll be creating magic in no time."

—Suzy Batiz, the chief executive and visionary officer of ~Pourri, The Makers of Poo~Pourri, supernatural, and Alive OS®

"Melissa's words are authentic and important. She is a great listener and now shares reality-based strategies for imagining your own imperfect, fulfilling life."

—Martha Hennessey, a former New Hampshire State Senator/Member of the House of Representatives

"This is the book for a mom who wants a second jet engine to embark on her own journey from thinking she will have to wait another lifetime to dream big to knowing she can take steps right now to uncover and do what she would find more fulfilling at this life stage. Melissa writes both intimately and conversationally about topics that many moms around the world can relate to (some dads too). She invites the reader into a personal and deep journey about topics that are crucially important to uncover what would make a mom truly happy to work on...even after the kids are in bed. It was an honor and a pleasure to speak with her for an interview, which she has included excerpts of in this book, too!"

—Ken Honda, Japan's best-selling Zen millionaire and the author of *Happy Money: The Japanese Art of Making Peace with Your Money*

"The pandemic was an opportunity for so many of us to reevaluate, course-correct and grow. Coming out of it now, this book can help us all reimagine and reset. I especially love the hilarious, poignant stories about motherhood in today's society and the window into the psyche of people who go for it and get it done. There's inspiration on every page."

—Macollvie Neel, a communications executive in Brooklyn, New York

"The words imagination, play, and fun are not the usual things we as mothers think of when wondering how to get a grip back on our career, and I believe this book provides a really fresh take and lots of food for thought for mothers reading it. Its tone is so energetic and fresh!"

—Alejandra Molina, a coach in Miami

"Melissa is a mom of three with big dreams who tells it like it is. She draws on her own experiences and the experiences of professionals she's interviewed for her podcast to reflect on the plight of the mother. How do women conform to or challenge the traditional 'mom script'? If you're a mom, what can you do to break the 'cultural glass ceiling' to be yourself and a great parent, all without having to force yourself into a mom mold that doesn't fit you? Melissa is like a great friend, honest and wise and funny, telling you about her life and asking you to reflect on yours. This book is a great purchase for moms in every stage of life."

—Maureen Turner Carey, a librarian in Austin, Texas

"In her book, Melissa shows us that motherhood does not have to be a pause or an end to your pre-child(ren) self. With guidance from her podcast guests, she encourages us to think big, find what lights us up, and move toward our goals with the steps that fit the reality of our lives today. In doing so we honor and inspire our child(ren) and our own inner child."

—Katherine Howell, a museum administrator in Queens, New York

FERTILE IMAGINATION

Fertile IMAGINATION

A GUIDE for STRETCHING EVERY MOM'S SUPERPOWER for MAXIMUM IMPACT

MELISSA LLARENA

First paperback edition October 2023

Book cover design by Jasmine Hromjak
Book interior by Sarah Lahay
Editing by Amanda McMahon
Copyediting by Laura Carney

ISBN 979-8-9885286-0-9 (paperback)
ISBN 979-8-9885286-1-6 (ebook)
ISBN 979-8-9885286-2-3 (hardcover)

Published by Unimaginable Publishing House

www.fertileideas.com

Special discounts for bulk sale are available for book clubs, mom groups, and organizations.

Please contact melissa@fertileideas.com

Before you start retracing your steps to reawaken, play with, and stretch your imagination, you may want to take a free quiz to check your Imagination Wellness Assessment. This is especially useful if you are not where you want to be as an ambitious mom with entrepreneurial goals. It's on my website. You'll also have the opportunity to download the Imagination Warm-Ups Playbook while you are there. You are encouraged to complete the prompts after each chapter for maximum impact. Enjoy this printable format to enhance your personal reflection or as a group discussion guide amongst your mom friends in a book club setting. The original podcast interviews featured in this book, immersive resources to nurture your imagination, and my latest updates are all online at:

www.fertileideas.com

Most importantly, you'll also want to join the **Imagination to Impact Five-Day Challenge** (valued at $49, yours for free) to reawaken, play with, and stretch your imagination to discover your most fertile idea. This is where to start to experience firsthand what using your fertile imagination can look like in your daily life with your kids.

DEDICATION

To my Cuban abuela, Anna Luisa: your legacy is one of unimaginable proportions. I'm grateful that you were brave enough to use your fertile imagination to nurture mine. Some of my most fertile ideas have flourished, while others are still at the seedling stage, such as my three sons, for whom I am brave.

CONTENTS

PREFACE

REDISCOVERING MY FERTILE IMAGINATION FUELED MY TWO-YEAR WRITING JOURNEY

THERE'S A BACKSTORY TO every story. (You have one, too, right?) When I was a little girl, every night I would imagine myself doing something brave or just wonderful. One night I was in a breakdancing performance and taking home the top prize. Another I was reunited with my first kiss. My imagination helped ease my way into sleep. I relied on my imagination for visions of myself doing incredible things because those visions inspired me. I once imagined myself screaming out my window that I'd been admitted to an Ivy League school. There were also moments I let myself get so lost on a playdate with my imagination that I pretended I was living in London. I have so much to be grateful for when it comes to my very fertile imagination, including those moments when it was just us navigating my mom's battle with manic depression. Me and my imagination—we were inseparable.

Then something happened. I became a mom. I brought home my firstborn from the hospital. He was not a good sleeper. (Was yours?) In my early motherhood days, I didn't have that "imagining time" between placing my head on the pillow and falling asleep. I'd drop on the mattress and pass out. My imagination didn't stand a chance. Then, when I had identical twins, the only thing I could rely on each night during that first year was feelings of overwhelm and dread. Was I going to make it? How would I survive another sleepless night? It was official by this point, I had lost my imagination—a once reliable friend and resource and the source of my audacious goals and big dreams. Several years passed where I couldn't even force myself to imagine something incredible for myself or visualize what would be possible in my life because being a mom to three boys felt like a cap had been placed on my dreams. Instead, I forced myself, with very little energy, to move through my business, life, and sometimes motherhood. Could I ever bring my imagination back?

This book is proof that I found a way to reawaken my own imagination and so can you. Right before I began writing this book, I had a vision that captivated me again. I saw myself in the Great Library of Alexandria in Egypt placing this book on a library shelf. As a proud library card holder at libraries around the world, including in London, where I **did** get to live (recall that initial vision of me living there that I had as a child?); at Dartmouth, where I eventually earned my graduate degree (another idea I'd had in childhood—that envisioned window scream); and approximately 10 other locations, I saw my book done and nestled on shelves for others to read. This vision that came from my imagination sustained me during what became a two-year writing journey, which included massive life interruptions and change. (If you're a mom, you know how much can happen in a two-year timespan! Am I right?) We globally relocated from Australia to the U.S. If you've never made that kind of a family move, then just recall when you had your first child or expanded your family in other ways... it means lots of interruptions, adjustments, uncertainty, and sleepless nights. Yet, throughout those two years, I made a commitment to play with my imagination. I didn't want to lose it again. Writing this book is the ultimate stretch of my imagination because it's me asking **you** to use your imagination to see the greatness in yourself, which is exactly what I always hoped my mom could do.

INTRODUCTION

LESSONS IN AN IMAGINATION SUPERPOWER FROM MY PODCAST GUESTS AND ME

WHOEVER THOUGHT "MOM JEANS" would be in style again? You know the ones—they seem to rise up to your armpits. When I see them on young, childless girls, I squint to see if I can imagine them looking remotely cool on me. My Puerto Rican ass would fill the entire real estate of their extra-long height, from crotch to above my navel area. I'm not yet convinced this will look flattering. Can I pull it off? My waist is small, especially for someone who has three sons. I'm still curious if I could make mom jeans look unmom-like. I never imagined that moms could set trends for anyone without kids!

I have filled the past eleven years with a mental game, to see just how unmom-like and sometimes unMelissa-like I can design my life. I wanted to reframe what I'd seen or been told a mom should be. What about all of the other identities I had before becoming a parent? Was I relegated to burying them along with my placenta back in 2011? My desire to not act like a mom is making for a magnificent life. It's enhanced my family's experiences and expanded what they think is possible too. As I reflect on the crazy things I've done, and continue to do, I'm feeling kind of confident that perhaps I can "work it" in mom jeans. Even if it's only in my imagination. Seemingly, mine has gotten quite fertile.

A sense of wonder, access to wisdom, limitless energy, a willingness to dream, and a playful spirit culminating in bursts of daily fulfillment. This book is for moms who want them back! Maybe it's been awhile since you've felt like you were bursting out of your skin with hope and expectancy, with your own ambitions? If this is the case, then I have great news for you! You are in the right place.

This book is for moms who refuse to buy into the BS that being a mom means stomping on their personal ambitions unless they are directly tied to the happiness of their kid/s. Once you relied on your dreams and big ambitions to feel alive. Your dreams may have been your life force; heck your dreams may have made you bounce out of bed without an alarm clock! This book is for you, if you feel you have lost the greatest parts of your before-kids life. If this is where you are today then I want to help you transform; from feeling limited by your inherited motherhood "scripts" to being excited and thrilled by life. Imagine feeling as jacked up (in a good way) for yourself as you do when your least athletic kid scores a goal at soccer one glorious

Saturday. You deserve to feel that wide-eyed, hopeful, and tickled hot pink about the possibilities. This is the book I needed when I paired motherhood with entrepreneurship eleven years ago. In my case, I was so desperate to hang onto my pre-mom dreams and desires that I determinedly set out to discover what I could do, even if that meant bringing my kid squarely attached to my nipple to a prospective client meeting. I'll save that story for later.

I'm convinced moms may have just misplaced these things along with their house keys. Chances are you can find them by retracing your steps. The best way to achieve this is to engage an imagination: your own, the ones around you, or your kids', in new, unexpected yet practical ways. Ways that fit for us moms whose minds are full of internal dialogue and need a spark to untangle what matters most. Since 2011, as a coach to many moms, untangling what matters most has meant helping them decipher what other people expected of them and what they really wanted for themselves. Once this knot is smoothed out it becomes possible for my clients to focus on how best to use their distinguishable gifts for maximum impact. This clarity inspires my clients to then share their ideas with other people. As I reflected on the specific ways that worked for me along with the key lessons I tailored into my life, I uncovered my signature method of coaching both myself and others. My **Imagination to Impact Method**™ includes three stages, into which I've divided this book. You can follow them sequentially or skip ahead.

Let's walk through the three stages to rediscover and fuel your fertile imagination.

A fertile imagination can cast a powerful and compelling vision that will drive you to turn it into your reality even if it's never been imagined as possible for mothers before. It produces fertile ideas whose impact can transcend generations. This superpower is versatile—it has revitalized flat-out tired moms to enable them to tandem-nurse twins for one year; it has come up with unexpected strategies that have helped creative entrepreneurs bounce back; and it has helped generate visionary ideas to sustain the pace necessary to lead massive global efforts.

The route to your fertile imagination can be found by **first** focusing on ways to reawaken your imagination, which takes building awareness of why it's been missing (or more like hibernating) along with why it might not want to wake up. A fertile imagination requires a favorable environment to sprout its best ideas. You'll want to set your internal environment in particular, for the greatest possible harvest.

Second, once you've revived your original playdate, you will play with your imagination. You'll have ample opportunities to engage it in novel and unexpected ways to uncover what you'd like to experience more of in your life. The key is to plant several seeds in the best environment possible to see which show signs of the greatest growth; in this case, growth includes feeling positive emotions including excitement and presence—essentially, experiencing what your kids feel when they are playing.

The **third** stage is to stretch your imagination. You want to create a maximum impact? This takes learning how to creatively gather the support of others so that you can make the biggest possible difference with your ideas. Imagine making a bigger mark on the world than you ever thought possible. There are seasons in motherhood. You may feel as if you've fallen behind on your ambitions during busy ones. This is why it's important to find ways or get tools so you can sprint toward your dreams during the steadier mom-life moments.

Your fertile imagination has its best shot at impacting future generations if you commit to experiencing all three stages to maximize your own impact. You want your kids to achieve greatness on their terms? The best path is to learn how to use your fertile imagination to achieve greatness on your terms first. Want to see what that looks like?

Within each stage, to help you tap into the power of your imagination, I am going to share some stories with you. You can expect to hear about my outrageous adventures; the result of unleashing my imagination and going for it. Some are the opposite of anyone's expectations of a mom with three school-age boys.

I've also included surprising stories from my podcast. I have been producing *Unimaginable Wellness* since 2017. It's a place where I explore, with my guests, a whole range of well-being topics aimed at supporting entrepreneurial moms who want more out of life. I have interviewed incredible people whose adventures and achievements were enabled by their chutzpah and very fertile imaginations. I'm going to tell you more about how I started my podcast as you read on, but as unexpected as it may sound, I believe us moms can learn a lot about achieving personal fulfillment and happiness from people who are not moms, not from our country of origin, outside of our socioeconomic group, and completely unfamiliar with our situation. I'm never going to suggest that non-moms get a say on how you should be a mom. My intention behind including non-moms is to challenge you to set aside the baggage that came with taking on your mom identity and talk about how to go to the edges of what is possible. The idea is for you to get buck naked; it should be okay for a mom to step away from the expectations of society, culture, and conventional thinking. I want to help you to have the best shot at reaching your fullest capacity on this planet. Some of my personal accomplishments, since becoming a mom, were never on my menu of options, based on what I was told. If I'm being honest, I've done some things that may be found on the kids' menu! You may never want to emulate some of my podcast guests and become a *New York Times* best-selling children's illustrator or make the *Forbes* list of self-made female millionaires, but their stories will inspire you. A fertile imagination is a resource. You will **see** how others have harnessed its power. As a mom, can't you use all the resources you can get? I can! I have curated these stories because I was able to relate to them. I learned from them, and, if you keep an open mind, I promise you will too. None are telling you how to mother. Instead, you will see a fuller picture of how people are finding their own fulfillment and happiness in their lives.

The only tool you'll need is your superpower—your fertile imagination. The permission I am gifting you is this: use it to propel you toward your dreams. You will uncover why, as a mom, you should give *yourself* the permission to use this superpower.

You can jump into any chapter that you might need, at the moment. This book was written for moms who can appreciate that reading an entire book in one uninterrupted, cozy sitting is as rare as finding two 100-sheet, wide-ruled, red-covered composition notebooks at Walmart a week before school begins. If you're having a "I can't go to the bathroom without company" kind of day, then just read some journal questions to get your engines going; meditate on them, even if you don't have the time to read the chapter. **You can also download the Imagination Warm-Ups, e.g., journal prompts, right here: www.fertileideas.com (it's a shortcut)!** The idea is this: Just like those crystals you can buy at woo-woo stores, when you look at my chapters, see if one calls to your attention. Start there—you truly can choose your own adventure. I trust that you will know what you need, when you need it, and be able to make this wisdom your own.

However, if you are a nerd like me, then read it sequentially. Meditate and journal using the questions at the end of each chapter. Then take a dive, implement that chapter's one key idea, consistently, for one week. You might be an active reader like me. Break out the highlighters and stickers. Make it a thing. In my life, the ideas in this book lifted me (and other moms) up, and they can do the same for you!

It's time to use your fertile imagination to *really* make a difference.

I.

REAWAKEN YOUR IMAGINATION

IN THIS FIRST SECTION we will focus on reawakening your imagination. You need an alert imagination to produce fertile ideas. You need fertile ideas every day. There is no optimal window of time for when you can wait for them; some ideas have to launch during precise times or their optimal harvesting season will end. Even mom jeans had on- and off-trend moments. As for your imagination, I wish it could just wake up without the need for so much hoopla or caffeine. However, it needs some help. Before you truly stretch your imagination to make great things happen you need to warm it up. With the help of my podcast guests I will describe the dynamics at play when a woman rethinks her post-kids life. Is your imagination in hibernation because of cultural influences and societal expectations? Should being a mom or a woman limit what you can imagine being possible in your life? Did your mind prefer that you let go of your dreams permanently when you took on motherhood? Maybe your imagination has been neglected for so long that it's unwilling to show up under those conditions. Perhaps it's lost in some Guatemalan rainforest and hiking alone, so to wake it up sounds scary.

We will set out all the things that may be holding you back and my guests and I will share with you ways we have overcome them. Most of my guests have children, so they get it. Some aren't parents, but they still have great insights every mom can learn from. All throughout this section, you also have me by your side, sharing my hiccups as a mom, podcaster, and entrepreneur, as well as some of my greatest accomplishments with my three sons in tow.

Before you start reawakening your imagination, make sure to download the Imagination Warm-Ups in a printable workbook format for personal reflection or as a group discussion guide amongst your mom friends from my website. A free quiz to know your Imagination Wellness Assessment is also there. It will help you as a creative mom figure out: where to focus to give the best of yourself to your business and kids. The results might surprise you. You'll also find the original podcast interviews featured in this section, mindfulness resources to nurture your imagination, and a link to my 100-day, 67K-word writing journey to land Gary Vaynerchuk on my podcast, not to mention my latest updates, at:

www.fertileideas.com

Most importantly, you'll also want to join the **Imagination to Impact Five-Day Challenge** (valued at $49, but yours for free) to reawaken, play with, and stretch your imagination to discover your most fertile idea. This is where to start to experience firsthand what using your fertile imagination can look like in your daily life with your kids.

Chapter 1

SHATTER CULTURAL GLASS CEILINGS
-JANE EGERTON-IDEHEN, A TECH EXECUTIVE

In this chapter you will:

- Consider if you might be reliving your mom's experience, even a sliver of it
- Explore how our ideas about being a mom are influenced by our culture
- Untangle the expectations you are living up to and decide which ones to release
- Examine how you want to play out your life beyond being a mom
- Think about the role models we observe and who influences our lives
- See that you're not alone in questioning why your ambitions have to take a back seat when you become a mom!

JANE EGERTON-IDEHEN was born in a slum in Lagos, Nigeria. Her surroundings were different from mine. I am a second-generation New Yorker. Yet hearing about Jane on my podcast gave me the distance I sometimes need to make sense of my own life. Is this ever the case for you? Until I was sixteen, my two significant role models were my grandmothers. I would spend my summer months with them, one month each. Neither believed in air-conditioning. Both lived in boiling-hot towns—the Cuban one in Miami and the Puerto Rican one in Ponce, Puerto Rico. You have never experienced humidity until you've visited either place. Imagine a little girl waiting at a Miami bus stop alongside her umbrella-carrying grandmother. We'd wait for what felt like days at a gas station for the bus to take us to Sears or the bank. The bus was often not air-conditioned. The final destinations were. This is why I still LOVE visiting banks. As a young girl, I was taught several things about being a woman. According to them, we needed to be married to a guy in the same way we needed our arms—this was essential. If I didn't get married, then what the heck would I be doing? The thought of not getting married was totally absurd to both my grandmothers.

My Cuban grandmother, my favorite abuela, would constantly tell me that someday I'd need to maintain my house. Watching TV wouldn't fly if it meant I'd skipped doing household chores. She'd tell me when I was a six-year-old that a man would leave me if I didn't learn how to pick up after myself. What she really meant was, if I didn't clean after both myself and my husband. One day, being my cheeky self, I said to my grandmother: that man wouldn't be right for me.

My grandmother was born on a farm in 1910. She was one of eleven girls in a family of thirteen kids. All those girls had to help out, because their dad died shortly after the thirteenth child was born. Those two boys in the family must have had it really good if my grandmother accepted her lot in life, to clean up after everyone. My grandmother could read, as she attended school to eighth grade, but that was about it. She did want a different life for me so she encouraged me to become a professional, which was pretty modern for her. However, she also envisaged a professional as someone who knew how to look after a man and keep a tidy house as well. See, my grandmother inherited what I call a "mom script." It's similar to the script an actor is handed. Although I'm not an actor, except for that one time we'll get to later, I do know that some actors were born to play the roles in the scripts they were given. It's hard to imagine anyone but Jim Carrey playing *The Mask*, right? But, there are other scripts where the actor really has to contort herself or maybe even lose fifty pounds to play the role. **I see the rules, traditions, and expectations of motherhood like a script.** Some of us got scripts that were easier to play and there are those of us who feel like we have to run on a treadmill.

Both of my grandmothers worked as seamstresses in factories and my grandfathers were porters. In their respective but very different homes the women lightened their husband's load. It didn't matter if she had one or three kids or a home full of tenants. My grandmothers never mentioned anything about anyone lightening *their* loads. Somehow the guys got to keep their free, pre-dad selves as their kids grew up, but my grandmothers had to set aside their pre-mom selves and replace this identity with everything their spouses weren't interested in learning about or adding to their plates. The men had more choices than the women, even before becoming parents. My gut when I was a little girl knew to fight against that prognosis.

What sort of expectations did you grow up with? Ever get a sense that if you didn't do it all then you'd abandon your heritage?

I want to inspire you to reawaken your imagination and expect more from yourself. This goes back to our script. What seems impossible or forbidden to you because of gender expectations?

Expectations for women's ambitions outside the home were low in Jane's hometown of Lagos while the gender-based limitations she confronted as a child, teen, and young woman were high. Despite her origins Jane is now an engineer, who works for Meta and lives in Ireland with her family. She has a strong passion for promoting girls in STEM. She is also passionate about retaining and promoting women in STEM industries in Africa. She is also an author, having written what she calls a letter to her daughter, a book entitled: *Be Fearless: Give Yourself Permission to Be You.*

Let's see how Jane wrote her own script. It began with a challenge. This is when Jane's imagination came out to play. Jane recollects that moment when she was living in a slum in Nigeria:

> I just discovered that I was driven by challenge. I'd overheard my mom, having a discussion with an elderly friend who said she had a son studying engineering. He told her it was so difficult, and people are failing out of class. Few of them can graduate. She was just going on and on. I was eavesdropping, by the way. I told myself, yeah, that's what I want to do. The difficult one.

Jane was a child at the time. She also had an active imagination. At that moment, overhearing this conversation, Jane imagined she could become an engineer. Being strong in math, she knew she had evidence to support her plan. Her family pressured her to become a doctor (even this was light-years ahead of what Jane's peers were expected to do). But Jane wanted to push herself even harder. Perhaps, she thought, if most people failed in engineering school, I will need to be smarter.

As Jane told me her story I wasn't surprised by the lack of encouragement for a young, intelligent woman. What did shock me was how blatantly gender stereotypes played out in the workplace once Jane was qualified. During my decade as a coach I'd often heard about gender stereotypes in the workplace, but usually they were subtle. Remember what my grandmother said about being a woman? The stereotype she adhered to meant I could be a professional but at the same time and with the same level of dedication I also had to ensure my house was spotless.

Jane describes the kind of discrimination she experienced during a job interview in Nigeria.

> Sometimes it's clear-cut. I've sat in an interview and someone asked me:
>
> "Is your husband aware you're interviewing for this job?" I'm like, I think so. If I'm here, I guess he knows?
>
> "Do you know it requires a lot of travel? Does your husband know that?" I wanted to do the job because of the travel.

I was asked funny things like, "Do you have kids?" "How many kids do you have?" "Do you plan to have more kids?"

Jane mentioned in our interview how she shared this experience with her husband, who laughed and said he has never been asked these questions. Often these vastly different assumptions about the roles of women versus men in their careers and homelife are deep in our cultures. In some countries, such as the U.S., there are laws that make asking those kinds of questions illegal.

How is your "cultural" glass ceiling stopping you from being yourself? In my culture, I was expected to prioritize my housework; sweeping the dust on my floors must get done by me or I should feel shame for hiring help or leaving the dust there. Notice how my thinking doesn't even consider that perhaps my husband needs to pick up his own dust? Some of these cultural glass ceilings are deeply ingrained. I could be wheeling and dealing in my business, but no matter how tired I am or how big a business deal I bring in, that dust continues to pile up and I should feel anxious about it. My husband on the other hand doesn't even see the dust. It's not in his consciousness. He will feel zero anxiety even on his day off. I know this because I've asked him. It feels totally on purpose that he ignores it. I'll save my relationship advice for another lifetime, but it's important to examine these things.

So many of us, like Jane, pursued our education and competitive careers but then chose not to climb the career ladder. It's as if we think that if we stopped playing the gender role script that was handed down to us, there would be consequences—something might break. You may be living in the U.S., but your family came from somewhere with different female norms. Maybe you are Nigerian? The script is likely deeply ingrained in your thinking, despite where your feet might be planted today. Look at its roots. **You can break through this cultural glass ceiling when you recognize you are following parts of your "mom scripts" that are inauthentic or that you are striving to meet an unrealistic standard of perfection.**

Jane offers us this example:

> [In Nigeria] you would show up from work. Then you still have to be the domesticated wife. The man will probably show up from work and he doesn't have to do that. He just goes and lays on the couch. He expects his dinner to be served in a certain way, the home has to be cleaned in a certain way. All that work still hinges on the woman, with no support and it makes it tougher. Think about it. Cooking until 3 a.m. when you have a board meeting, because your husband insists you have

to be the one to cook the food. You may have to go and play the role of an executive that heads a multinational company. But tonight, you're going to cook, even though you can afford a cook.

You may not experience the same level of discrimination that Jane did in her career or have the same strict cultural expectations that were placed on me, but I want you to think about the stereotypes you think you need to conform to. You'll need a dose of self-awareness to uncover the lines you are reading from your own "mom script" and the courage to make the script your own.

Jane reflects on this:

That's just some belief system out there, set to hold you back. People don't know any better. It's not from a place of bitterness, or anger, or jealousy, especially because those beliefs might come from your relatives, your parents, people that are close to you, people that you respect, and that's why it's difficult. People don't know who you really are. But it's just good to ensure that girls are empowered to know that they can chase after their dreams, because they can be the next person to find the next big solution for world problems. Why do we have to limit things like solving a world problem to a certain gender?

Jane experienced several hiccups en route to becoming an engineer. She didn't have a neatly carved-out path. There was, however, a mentor who crossed her path and kept questioning her interest and knew how to push her buttons. A college administrator eventually convinced Jane to aim even higher.

You'll need guidance too. You'll have to rethink or reimagine your cultural identity. You may need to imagine being a woman who pushes herself beyond her family's limits. This will wake up your imagination and force you to think about what's possible for you.

Jane decided that once she broke the rules, she wanted to be sure those ceilings didn't close up again behind her. Jane was compelled enough to write a book while she was still juggling her roles as a wife, mom, and top sales executive.

What I thought in my head was, this is a letter to my daughter. That's the original title I gave it. I kept telling myself, what am I really trying to say to Sarah? I share a lot of experiences in the book that required me to be vulnerable. Not all of them were pleasant, some of them were tough. They're tough. [A lot of experiences were] really tough to put on paper because all the emotions come back. Once you're trying to recall moments then all the emotions come back. I really had to be sincere and transparent with her; it forced me to be courageous, to be vulnerable. I felt, if I'm telling Sarah I have to give her the best and tell the truth. I have to be very open, and share my emotions, what I learned, what I thought I could have done better, and what I did better with. So that's really the inspiration that drove me to write the book.

It's not only you who needs to learn these lessons. If you are going to challenge your script, then make sure you show your kids they can too. You get to be the matriarch of your generation and the next one. Jane has one son. I can see how her daughter was her first audience. I was curious how Jane approached this topic with her son. It's important for all genders to pick up the lessons women have learned.

Ultimately, as Jane suggests, all of society gets value when both men and woman can contribute at the highest levels of their potential. So this is what Jane did to get her son ready to be a stand-up partner to a wife or an ally to his sister or all women.

I made my son read the book. I want him to understand what it takes to have a woman in your life as a partner, as a sister, as a mother, and how he should see them. He should see them for who they are not just based on their gender. I think it is in sharing this message that we will determine the men we will have for the future. If we train our boys right then this determines how they will see women in the future, how they respect them in a partnership, in a relationship, in the office, you know, the perspective of them. So next time someone tells my son Asha, "Sarah can't do that because she's a girl," he can correct that person and say, "No," even if my daughter can say this herself. It has nothing to do with helping a girl. That's what I want him to understand. I think that would have been the best job I could have done.

The wrong script for you can hold you back. My Puerto Rican grandmother, who finished school after the third grade, got impatient with my mom back in the '60s. One of three girls, my mom attended a community college to earn her associate's degree. No other daughter went that far. My grandmother once told my mom, that's enough school! She saw school as a waste of time for a girl. Decades later, my mom enrolled in college because she really wanted to earn a bachelor's. The problem was that my mom was working full-time, I was born, and she had to complete all of her domestic duties for my father. No adjustments would be made to her script because my mom was carrying a full load of classes. My mom's anxiety levels, due to her duties of being the primary caregiver as a wife and mom on top of her studies, led her to quit. Imagine if my mom, before she met my dad or had me, could have called BS on her own mother? Lashing out at your mom in a Puerto Rican household in my mom's experience could result in a black eye, so bottling up disappointments was often a better option. The baby step to changing a script that doesn't feel true to you is in asking yourself the question: Is that behavior or expectation right for ME?

In a nutshell, you have an opportunity to reawaken your own imagination by challenging yourself to rewrite your script and break through a cultural glass ceiling. Find a challenge, like Jane did, that intrigues you. Is there anything holding you back? Do you need to break away from expectations? Figure out why this challenge is so compelling; you don't need to be like Jane and pursue it because it's hard. Hold that "why" close to your heart and use it as a focus. Imagine all the places you can go that your own grandparents told you never to be caught dead in.

On the other side of the spectrum, what if you were raised in an upper-middle-class house full of feminists who sparked your interest in advocating for women's rights and who told you that there was no glass ceiling you couldn't shatter? Let's see what other dynamics would be at play in that scenario in the next chapter. What if family teachings can overturn society's messaging?

Your turn to take what you've learned in this chapter to reawaken your imagination. Use the following section to tailor the lessons you've uncovered from this chapter to fuel your imagination this week.

BIG IDEAS

- Act like the matriarch of your generation and omit what no longer makes sense
- Be unafraid of challenging stereotypes of being a mom or a woman
- Know who you really are; it goes way beyond your lady parts
- Check in when you feel like you are acting like your own mom or other women in your family

IMAGINATION WARM-UPS

1. Think back to the gender-based limiting beliefs that irked you most as a kid. Imagine four or five of them.

2. Expand your thinking from the way those beliefs played out at home, in your community, at work, or elsewhere.

3. Think about two or three men in your life. What thoughts about how they spend their time working or days off have you had? Ever wanted to swap?

4. Quickly: brainstorm your own cultural glass ceilings that related to the role of a mother. Imagine the act of literally shattering one.

5. Think about the conversations that currently happen during family gatherings. Which ones feel more or less appropriate for moms to lead? Imagine how the tone may change if culturally it were more common for moms to lead those discussions?

Chapter 2

TACKLE YOUR DREAMS IN PHASES

-MARTHA HENNESSEY, A FORMER NEW HAMPSHIRE SENATOR/MEMBER OF THE HOUSE OF REPRESENTATIVES

In this chapter you will:

- Learn that you have a lifetime to achieve your dreams
- Stop thinking you aren't accomplishing enough
- Understand that you can make room for your dreams while mothering
- Acknowledge you don't have to do everything all at once but there is always something you can do
- Witness a woman who keeps evolving and making a bigger impact
- See that measuring yourself against others is a waste of energy

ARE YOU FRUSTRATED because you don't think you are achieving enough? Do you fantasize about having five lives? I bet you have a lot of priorities right now. I wish we could freeze time to work on our dreams and then care for our kids. However, you heard it here, sometimes we'll need to use our imagination to use our time wisely and prioritize executing our dreams. Conversations between moms often go like this: "I've heard our kids need us when they are babies, and I do not want to miss their first steps." "Then, in middle school, they'll need us to navigate their awkward years." "Then there are college applications." "I've heard kids' challenges grow as time goes on. So it seems like every stage is important!" Huh? So when is it time for you? This circuitous way of rationalizing putting yourself on the back burner is not new. In this chapter, you will see how these dynamics have existed for decades. This narrative has so much momentum; social media reinforces it by presenting an unrealistic image of what a good mom should look like.

The force is strong! So it's important you recognize it but thoughtfully plan how you will show up for yourself. Some of your dreams may have timestamps too. Ever try building a business? It's easier if you have one kid than three. Want to run a marathon in Berlin? A good time might be when the kids are teenagers and can appreciate the profundity of the place. Timing is everything for you too.

Ever thought about that? Maybe you shouldn't miss out on being thirty or forty or fifty either?

The key is not to throw up your hands and say, *F*ck it! I'm just going to ride this wave and hide while I'm knee-deep in dirty diapers.* Instead, this chapter will show you how to plan to achieve your ambitions, ignore the haters who might tell you that you are not being a great mom, and let go of the guilt you've been conditioned to feel that the media has facilitated. You need to work out what ambitions are achievable for you now and consider how you will navigate being the mom you want to be too.

It's wise to find elders whose lives or accomplishments you admire because these motherly emotions are not new. Martha was the right messenger for me. She showed me how mom guilt was a waste of energy and that many things can be important in your life. Did you get that? This is where I want to give you hope. You may have several dreams today. However, you don't necessarily have to do everything in one shot. If you are like me then you may want to do a lot of things in your one life. You also don't need to stop when you "retire." Heck, you never have to retire. Martha didn't. It's time to find out more about Martha Hennessey. She will help you reimagine how many dreams you can achieve in one life.

When I attended the Tuck School of Business at Dartmouth, I lived in Martha's apartment. She was my landlord. I hadn't planned on getting to know Martha quite as well as I did. However, one weekend I didn't lock an outside door entirely and a water pipe burst. There was water everywhere, causing a lot of damage.

So, this accident is why Martha and I REALLY got to know each other. We were at the Dirt Cowboy café on Main Street. The hot topic of the moment was about how I was going to cover the damages I was responsible for. Thank God Martha was super compassionate with me. We split the bill, as she had landlord insurance. Once we had dealt with the damages our conversation expanded into life in general. I'm sure we had already agreed to split the damages by then, because I felt comfortable enough to change the topic and discuss something personal with a stranger.

Between nervous sips of a cappuccino, I confessed to Martha that eventually I wanted to be a mom. I shared with her that I wasn't sure how to be a working mom. To which she told me: No mom regrets the time she gets to spend with her child.

I had been married for four years by that time and I was running out of excuses for not having kids. I knew I had to figure the working mom thing out eventually. Fast-forward to today; there have been many days when Martha's lesson has comforted me. Has that ever happened to you? You stumble upon a wise soul who tells you just what you need to tell yourself years later? I couldn't have imagined that I was ever going to leave my corporate job when I became a mom. Back then, Martha had the perfect words.

This brings me to how we reconnected and Martha's podcast episode. I was living in Sydney, Australia, when I noticed a Facebook post celebrating Martha's success in public office. She served in the New Hampshire Senate 5th district from 2016 until 2020; she had also previously served on the Children and Family Law Committee in the New Hampshire House of Representatives from 2014 to 2016. It felt like a sign for me to reconnect with her, more than a decade after our Dirt Cowboy Café chat. The circumstances in which we now found ourselves were worlds apart from that time. I was a mom to three young boys and Martha was a grandmother. Martha never forgot me. (*I wonder why?*) When we began the interview, we focused on her political career, but then halfway into it we delved into motherhood. This is when things got passionate for the two of us.

It became clear that the issues that moms struggle with traverse the decades. I shared with Martha what I saw during the pandemic. Many moms were struggling. A lot of us were on the brink of breaking. Our anxiety was at an all-time high. Working moms had to homeschool. Stay-at-home-moms felt as if they were drowning. The consequences of dealing with the virus were like an atomic bomb on our sanity. We were already juggling glass balls in the air, before the pandemic. Then when the schools and childcare solutions imploded it was like some asshole was throwing more and more balls at us. Think more like a baseball pitching machine that broke.

Here is what Martha had to say about juggling glass balls.

> When I was finishing my doctoral dissertation, we put our two very young children into a family daycare center that we could barely afford. I remember sitting at home, feeling guilt and some kind of shame that I wasn't with my children. And yet, when they came home, I was feeling resentment about the fact that I couldn't get my work done. So you're in a position where you feel like you can't win, especially as a mother, but as any mother or father.

It was so reassuring to hear her express the same dilemma I was experiencing. Can you see why I admire Martha and have held onto her wisdom through the years? **This is the struggle all moms face, finding a path between caring for our children and fulfilling our own dreams that we can live with.** There is nothing more beautiful than a mother who is happy about her own life, but sometimes this takes courage and persistence. It may mean you need to look carefully at what works for you now and remember you don't need to achieve everything today. Don't look to others to work out what you should be doing, focus on what works for you. Especially don't look to others to tell you what a good mom looks like. Martha could see her daughter who is an OB/GYN struggling too during the pandemic.

> I finally said to my daughter, you know, everyone on social media is telling you that you should never let your children watch television. Well, I'm here to say, again, that many people have been brought up watching *Sesame Street* and other carefully screened television programs and gone on to live very good lives. The only way as a working mother that I could make a meal was to have my children watch *Sesame Street*, for example. I probably didn't talk about it, because in my mind, they [other moms] were all at home, making cooking a meal into a learning project with their children or some such thing. That wasn't my reality at all. It certainly isn't the reality that our children are now confronting as parents. So we have to stop parent shaming.

We will need to adjust the goalposts from time to time. There will be days when you will not complete your to-do list. Set aside the frustration on those days. You need your energy. These feelings are energy vampires: frustration, resentment, shame, and guilt. You can use your imagination to figure out how to process those emotions. You don't need to carry your emotions with you all day long, and remember, you have a lifetime to achieve things.

> At the end of the day, looking in the mirror and saying, I should have gotten this accomplished, I should have gotten that accomplished, I should be a better parent, and I should be at work longer hours is not productive. How about if we could magically replace it with: I did a pretty good job under the circumstances. I had a lot on my plate and all the things I had on my plate were important. I'm okay with the fact that my children watched two hours of TV today, because I was careful to ensure they watched something that wasn't going to scar them for life. By making that allowance it allowed me to do things that are important in a different part of my life. So, you know, maybe it's enough to say: I was enough today, I did enough today, and not focus on what I should have done.

See this is why I listen to Martha. She's my working-mom spirit guide. She hasn't let mom guilt or society's expectations hold her back. Martha is a lifelong learner. Her psychology career could have been her endgame, but when she was in her sixties she decided to get into politics. She's a great example of how you can achieve many things in your lifetime.

Let's take Martha's words to heart here. You may have several interests today. You may also have several kids. So how can you prioritize one of your dreams? What can you do to fit it into your everyday life? Are there times in your day when you can listen to podcasts? Or listen to audiobooks? Or narrate your book into an audio recording device as you get your 10K steps in your day? I double-duty a lot. When I drive or do the groceries I listen to podcasts. What can you do during that time? Get imaginative. Then, like Martha, if your dreams are important, which they are, figure out a longer trajectory for yourself. You can devote one year to one dream or do it by the decades.

In my case, my first dream was to open a coaching business online. My firstborn was six months old when I opened my LLC. I wanted to open my doors right away, and my first client was a former colleague's husband. The evening before I went to my very first business meeting I opened up a Microsoft Word document and made up my pricing and services. My big-ticket item was $1,000. I had no childcare. So, in true New York fashion, I put on my Ergobaby carrier and headed to Midtown on a train. We met at a bakery. My friend was there with her husband. She agreed to carry my cute son while I spoke with her aspiring investment banker husband. Twenty minutes into my pitch, my colleague frantically told me: "Melissa, Gabriel looks uncomfortable." **Something smelled. It was not the croissants. My baby had pooped on my client's wife.** I was mortified. My diaper change game was not at pro status yet. So awkward. However, when you are a mom on a mission, there just is no good time to start working on your dreams. When I think about the last ten years of my career, I feel like I've been hanging by a thread between one diaper blowout and another. While you can phase your dreams and set the groundwork even when you are in the thick of it, what if you start to neglect yourself in the process and something that cannot be fixed breaks? This is the reality of motherhood; the more kids you have, the more variables there are to manage. So how can you keep your eyes on the ball in the longer term while not neglecting yourself during some rough patches? This is addressed next by a Tupac-loving fifty-something-year-old DJ who went to hell and came back with a warning for moms who tend to forget they need to nurture themselves too.

Your turn to take what you've learned in this chapter to reawaken your imagination. Use the following section to tailor the lessons you've uncovered from this chapter to fuel your imagination this week.

BIG IDEAS

- Redefine what being a good mom means to you
- Your dreams are not lost if you can't tackle them all at once
- Seeking mom wisdom from moms outside of your family can be enlightening
- Keeping your eyes on the prize is not limited to your kid's or kids' happiness; your happiness is the prize too
- You are not behind; it ain't over at all

IMAGINATION WARM-UPS

1. Use your imagination to come up with the perfect time and place to work on your first dream. Then brainstorm the crap out of that perfect moment. Always have backups.

2. Plan out your dreams. Consider which ones require the right timing. Spread them out. What if you focused on one per year or five years?

3. If you don't have a bucket list of dreams at this point yet then plan out the seasons of your life as a mom. Just mark those moments when you will be able to immerse yourself in new projects, such as when the kids go to school full-time or leave for overnight summer camp. In later chapters, you'll be reminded to return here to plug your dreams into those openings.

4. Imagine a new evening routine during which time you can feel like you've won the day. What good did you accomplish today? What worked today? Why? Come up with ways to entertain your kids. What are some educational options you can preselect now?

5. Reimagine what being a good mom is for you.
   We are bombarded with commercials that are
   telling us what we should be aspiring toward,
   but have you ever given it any thought?
   What kind of mom do you want to be?

Chapter 3

AVOID TAKING YOURSELF FOR GRANTED

-FIFTY-YEAR-OLD DJ "YOUR MAMA" ESTHER GOEDVOLK

In this chapter you will:

- See what it takes to go from looking after others' needs to saying *I shouldn't f*ck with my needs anymore*

- Remember you only live once (YOLO); make it your mantra

- Explore how prioritizing your happiness is not being selfish

- Learn the danger of not looking after yourself; your body doesn't care about the reasons

CURIOUS? HOW ARE YOU taking yourself for granted? It's a loaded question because I haven't met one mom who hasn't done this at least once, and for some of us, it backfires. I speak from experience. I have pushed myself too. I always thought if I was sick, regardless of the symptoms, I could "will" my way back to health in twenty-four hours. Interesting how our imagination thinks of worst-case scenarios for our loved ones when they are sick but totally ignores us. Your needs shouldn't have to wait until everyone else is taken care of.

Back when I was house hunting in Connecticut, I delayed finding the perfect local doctor for myself. My thinking was simple: I can wait to find a doctor for myself until we find our permanent neighborhood and move into our home. Of course I ensured my kids had primary care pediatricians, but for me, it was okay to skip my annual visit to the doctor. Talk about self-neglect. I let one cold go pretty far before I realized it was more than just a cold. I wouldn't have waited nearly as long for any of my kids. My slight cough evolved into a rough one. I had a hard time speaking to mortgage lenders let alone my clients. It was that bad. It wasn't until I felt a pain in my lung that finally I hopped in a cab to head back to New York City to see my former doctor. It cost me over $100 and took more than an hour to drive to see him. When he heard my lung's crackle, he said, "**Melissa, this is the real thing. You have**

pneumonia." I was scared. Thank goodness all I had to do was pop some penicillin to recover, but that was enough for me to start to really care about my health. Meanwhile, if my sons have lice on their heads I take them to a world-class dermatologist. Go figure?

Our imagination can anticipate extraordinary bodily harm in those we care for. Some of us tend to sacrifice our bodies because we don't consciously imagine the same harm happening to us. Our fertile imagination deludes us into thinking we are unbreakable. We push ourselves farther than we should. Have you ever considered your imagination can also resurrect you when you've gone too far?

This brings me to Esther.... "We all wish we could be like Esther," one of my coaching clients said to me after Esther appeared as one of my podcast guests. Hers is the only EXPLICIT episode I have ever aired. Listening to Esther curse was just too darn cute and unexpected. She was definitely the writer of her own life script.

Esther Goedvolk is a DJ, in her fifties, based in Amsterdam. She goes by the professional name of DJ *Je Moeder* ("Your Mama"). Esther can spin Tupac or New Order and look just as confident for both. She's the type of woman who will show up to a DJ class meant for twenty-year-olds and be open to learning from them. She's worth learning from too, for a myriad of reasons. Only a few years earlier Esther had been caring for her daughter, who had been diagnosed with cancer at six. Because Esther was so focused on her daughter, she neglected her own health. Any caregiver, any mother knows how slippery this slope can be. We often take our health for granted while we care for someone else—our parents, partners, kids, clients, teammates, and even pets. It's almost like we play this game with ourselves. *How far can I take this?* We wouldn't play this game with our loved ones. What's stopping us from seeing ourselves as worthy of nurturing too? How does our imagination play a role?

The time Esther was caring for her sick daughter was stressful. She was hands-on. What mother wouldn't be?

In Esther's own words:

> You have to know yourself. You have to get to know your body. You have to look at yourself from a different perspective. I found out that most of the time I was doing too much. I didn't take care of myself. I just went on and on and on.

Esther was plagued with insecurities because she didn't know why she was in pain, but eventually, three years later, Esther herself was diagnosed with a rare form of cancer. What followed was a range of medical treatments and she was glued to the bed for three years. Three years! One treatment, a surgery, resulted in her not being able to feel her tailbone that entire time. Esther was chuckling during our interview because, as she pointed out, she behaved like the "Wicked Witch of the North" and thankfully she delegated things to her husband. Who knows what she was imagining during that time in her life? Imagine being in unbearable chronic pain for three years without knowing how you will ever live a normal life again? It sounded to me like that was the toughest pill to swallow for DJ *Je Moeder*. Ultimately, she decided to visualize a different prognosis and sought a more holistic approach to healing herself. Here's how Esther's story offers us a better appreciation for the power of our imagination even when we've neglected ourselves more than we should have.

Esther began to think about and believe in her ability to be bigger and greater than her diagnosis. She admitted herself into a holistic medical institute where she could focus on achieving this. She used her imagination to mentally distance herself from her diagnosis and pain. **Once you distance yourself from anything, it is then that you can see it, inspect it, and tweak it. It is then that self-healing can take shape.** The alternative is to own your diagnosis or pain. Esther believes, if you "are" your disease then it's harder to see and harder to cure it. So once you distance yourself from it you can imagine a reality where your life is no longer dictated by your diagnosis. This is an exceptional use of a mom's imagination in action. Esther did that. She became her own health advocate by seeking out the best help for herself.

It took imagination and emotional courage for Esther to explore alternative treatments. At one point, she had been taking fifteen medications every day. It was up to her to decide that she wanted out of her predicament. Imagine someone who is low on energy and in pain deciding to wean herself off of medications and use her mindset to heal? On the surface, it may sound crazy. Yet, this demonstrates how imaginative we all can be when we are desperate. Esther got creative and curious enough to explore alternative avenues to managing her health. She found an expert with a different approach, Dr. Joe Dispenza. He wrote the book, *You Are the Placebo*, in which he shares how to use mindset to heal physical ailments. Could our minds be that powerful? Let Esther's story be a testament to your innate power and ability to heal if things ever get out of hand for you.

One day Esther was doing one of Dr. Dispenza's breathing exercises when she began to feel her tailbone, which she had not felt in three years. She went on to later walk again and is in remission from her cancer. I am not recommending this approach will work for everyone who has cancer, but I wanted to show how Esther found a way to imagine herself healthy, hold onto that vibe, and not f*ck herself up. This is how Esther thinks about how we ignore our own needs:

> I think you only get f*cked up yourself when you don't do what you like to do. You're here to be happy. I think that's true. I think you're in the world to be happy. It sounds simple. You're not here to make other people happy; well, maybe sometimes. But when you're not happy, you're not loving yourself that much. I think you have a problem. I think you need to love yourself first, then you can love others.

When you look at Esther's circumstances, it's logical to see how she ignored her own health. Her reason was valid. However, our bodies are not going to give us a pass for ignoring them because our reasons for our neglect are valid.

It's clear that often we f*ck ourselves up when we live for others rather than for ourselves. We all need to use our imagination at some point or another to self-heal. So stop neglecting yourself and bring a healthy sense of imagination to your circumstances. You'll want to be open to new ideas and get really curious about alternative options. Let's do this.

Imagine for a minute that you loved yourself. I know. What a crazy thought experiment for a mom. What if you did everything in your power not to f*ck yourself? Hard to imagine, right? We think so much about others that sometimes I wonder if we even have the mental bandwidth to give ourselves some mindshare. When Esther was healed she enrolled in that DJ course where she was "knighted" with her DJ name, *Je Moeder*. When I was preparing for my interview with Esther, I thought we would be focusing on her badassery; to be in her fifties and DJ-ing foul-language tunes. As it turned out, Esther taught me something totally unexpected about myself and what could lie ahead if I continued to neglect myself. See, when I interviewed Esther I was forty-one years old. Esther had been diagnosed with cancer at forty-eight. "Esther" is also my mom's name, so the whole interview felt like some kind of synchronicity. What if Esther's story came as a warning to me? Was I f*cking myself up? Where in my life was I putting loving other people ahead of loving myself? Was I ignoring my health in any way? Esther's story prompted me to get really curious about my priorities. Was I even on my list at the time? Here's your chance: what's your priority today? Are *you* there?

My time living in Sydney was one of healing. I enlisted the help of all sorts of experts to help me with my physical and mental health. I think it's the whole idea of turning forty that sets you in one of those gears—I'm going to live my best life or I'm throwing in the towel. Seeing both of my parents suffer physically and one mentally has led me to opt for living my best life. My focus has been on preventative measures so I can live pain-free when I'm in my seventies. My mom is in pain all day, every day, even after surgeries and medicines. My dad has both a defibrillator and pacemaker just to make his heart work. The guy is also overweight, so his heart is technically trying to work for two people.

I also sought the help of a mental health professional to help me have the best shot at being an incredible mom. So much has been drilled into my head about inner child wounds and how they turn up in our adult lives, especially when we are in emotionally tumultuous moments. I would say being a mom to three boys who have their own ideas on how to interact and "play," i.e., proactively bug one another, qualifies as being tumultuous and trying every single day. I'd also add that my childhood resulted in many wounds and I would rather address them than pass them on.

I see my physical well-being and emotional well-being as being equally important; Esther's story shows us this is true. As the daughter of a mom with a mental illness, I've never lost sight that not all disabilities or illnesses can be seen. So in Sydney, with ample time and distance away from extended family obligations, I used my time to get to the gym four times a week no matter what and to see my therapist every month. I would have seen her weekly if it cost less.

Both priorities helped me find calm amidst the chaos of those last two years. I didn't seem to experience the same levels of anxiety as my friends in the U.S. because I managed to create a bubble for myself. It was an unintended blessing, as I was already en route to strengthening my mind and body when the pandemic came our way. If I hadn't been on my journey, then spending all that time alone with my thoughts and not having an energetic outlet for them during our lockdowns could have taken me down as it did many moms. When I got to Sydney, before the pandemic, I began fortifying my mind and body and that helped me stay on course and handle a lot. Of course, my husband was huge in all of this. I also had tools for when things felt scary, like the wildfires, and having to act during a moment of crisis right before the pandemic. If my body and brain had been suffering, taking action in that moment would have felt impossible...and then after the wildfires came the pandemic, which was a battle with uncertainty at its best....

Use your imagination as your salvo if things ever get out of hand. It's unlimited and can help you heal yourself physically and emotionally. Esther's story has a happy ending; however, what if you suffer an irreparable loss? We all experience big and smaller losses. Wouldn't it make sense to be proactive about readying yourself before they happen so you can handle them resiliently? Let's find out how a self-proclaimed adventurist mom approaches life's toughest challenges and puts herself through the gamut on purpose to get herself gladiator-ready for life's downs.

Your turn to take what you've learned in this chapter to reawaken your imagination. Use the following section to tailor the lessons you've uncovered from this chapter to fuel your imagination this week.

BIG IDEAS

- Don't f*ck yourself by doing things that make you unhappy
- Your body will break if you don't take care of it
- Self-neglect is a rather selfish thing because your family will have to pick up the slack
- Healing yourself may be an option if you believe in it enough
- It's okay to break the rules. YOLO.

\\\|//

IMAGINATION WARM-UPS

1. When was the last time you felt happy? Imagine what life could look like if you prioritized feeling happy once a day?

2. How can you come up with more imaginative and nourishing self-care practices in your daily life?

3. What if you could imagine yourself healthy the next time you got a cold?

4. What would it look like if you made a pact with your child (age-appropriate) to get your checkups together? What if you grabbed frozen yogurt to celebrate this new level of looking out for one another?

5. Imagine what a YOLO weekend could look like for you? Esther's daughter and now Esther are acting like they only live once. What would this weekend look like if this were your philosophy?

Chapter 4

FACE YOUR FEARS AND CHART A NEW COURSE

-MICHELLE GHILOTTI, THE FOUNDER OF MGI AND THE GREATER GOOD

In this chapter you will:

- See the opportunities you have to confront your fears and chart a new life course

- Explore becoming more resilient to get back up faster and set an example

- Realize that you don't need to escape real life to find your purpose

- Learn that you can continue to expand and grow even as you process any loss

- Witness how one mom rejected expectations of how she should grieve

WHAT SCARES YOU? I'm so afraid of heights that I can't even look at someone near the edge of a fenced rooftop patio. On my fortieth birthday, I decided to confront this fear. Months into living in Sydney, Australia, I was going to climb the Harbor Bridge. This is the bridge you may have seen on New Year's Eve with fireworks exploding. It's an iconic symbol of Australia. It reminds me of the Queensboro Bridge over the East River in New York City. Our climb was 439 feet high. There were vertical ladders to climb all the way up to its highest point so we could walk along its edges; it was not a casual stroll. The only thought that kept me calm was that David Hasselhoff had made the same climb and he's still around. It's a tourist attraction, not a death wish, and I was in a group of travelers, but nothing could have convinced my husband to join me. So I went alone and I opted for the steepest and more terrifying climbing package to ring in my new decade. I wanted to mark this time in my life with a newfound sense of bravery. I wasn't curious about what it would feel like to nosedive into Sydney Harbor but I was curious about what it would take to walk across without freaking out.

I had seen pictures of a local friend making the Sydney Harbor Bridge Climb—twice—and it made my stomach drop just looking at them. So when I first walked out onto a narrow, shaky wooden plank with a loose harness and a wrought iron handrail I came up with a mind-numbing rhythm to get through the entire experience. The beat was simple: feel the butterflies, then walk anyway. Repeat. I chose to remind myself with each step that I wanted this challenge on my fortieth birthday to face my fear of heights, I wanted to feel like I was doing something totally unlike "feet on the ground" me. I wanted to remember my fortieth as a day that I acted out of character...as a more adventurous mom. I didn't intend to conquer my fear at any point, but I wanted to feel my fear and do it anyway...really experience something that scares me and find a way to be okay in that moment and keep moving forward in my life...it was a test of sorts. If I could climb a bridge and coach myself through it then I knew I could apply the same experience, of how I wanted to change my life at forty, to other goals. I wanted to write a book...I needed to see if I could do new things.

There is a fear of meeting a challenge in all of us, especially when we choose to face our fears and change the script we think we should follow. **Before we start on our journey to build our imagination into a superpower we need to challenge and face the things that hold us back.** It is fear that often holds us back, especially the fear of stepping away from what is expected of us. For moms this is especially the case and we will look at lots of examples in this book. Martha Hennessey's decision to run for public office is not what you might expect from a retired grandmother.

You may think, what does this have to do with imagination? This brings me to my podcast guest Michelle Ghillotti. I had met Michelle, in what feels like another life, at a business conference in New York City before her life dramatically changed. I followed her online for many years and admired her honest accounts of life and her soulful stories. After our first meeting at that conference Michelle experienced two traumatic and sudden losses; her brother in his twenties in a car crash and later her mom. She used her imagination to not only face the fear of loss but also to challenge expectations of how we should grieve. She's a great example of someone who wanted to do things differently. Michelle was my first female guest. She once worked in advertising on the Nike and Starbucks brands. She is a "modern adventurist mom." She considers herself a serial expat who has lived in Mexico/Holland/U.S. As a business owner, she activates and supports socially active entrepreneurial women (or those aspiring to be) to make a tangible difference in the world through businesses-turned-movements. What stands out to me about Michelle is that she values relationships like no one I have ever met. She travels to see and hug all of her friends. She also makes time to volunteer in local prisons and has even gone to Syrian refugee camps. She's not afraid to look at life's pleasures and pains in the face, and I admire her for that. She's on a path to becoming a death doula now.

When I interviewed her for my podcast she told me about her journey after experiencing such tragic loss:

> I was healing those parts of me that essentially needed to be healed, by two things: by my creativity, because our creativity leads us to passion, which leads us to purpose, and also by connection to community. I could have stayed at home. I could have done [it] right. But, and it gives me chills again, [it takes] courage to follow what feels like the unnatural path. In other words, to follow expansion when all you want to do is recoil, when all you want to do is stay small or stay put or sit on the couch or lie in your bed.

Michelle let her imagination guide her healing journey. She decided not to recoil when her brother passed away. Wait? That's not in the script? In Michelle's case, she decided not to follow the script that says we should eject ourselves from the world as a sign of respect for those who are no longer in it. The biggest thing I admire about Michelle is the fearless way in which she challenged the expectations of how we should grieve. It's expected that when someone passes we should wear black. We assume that everybody mourns the same way or should do. Let's think about the script we might have been given as moms or humans.

Michelle has tried all sorts of things from swinging on a trapeze to fasting alone in the woods for days; this was years after their deaths. There's this spirit of conquering in Michelle that I admire. She has chosen to proactively conquer her fear of loss and grief rather than let it conquer her psyche, joy, or time on Earth. She is living proof of the benefits of proactively choosing your adventures. She has decided to train herself for the challenges of a well-lived life, which include grief, sadness, hardships, and even intense belly laughs.

Michelle says:

> We experience loss all the time, it doesn't have
> to be the loss of a physical person. There's
> discomfort, there's challenges [even] in looking
> for a job or saying yes to one. There is healing, if
> you're able to follow your creativity. I continue
> to follow my creativity. I continued...I kept the
> doors of my business open...as both these beloved
> beings of mine passed...I thought maybe I should
> just table things, table my projects. Then I said
> no; there's just something in me that said no, let
> me just see what it feels like to open the door
> to this new creative idea. Let me just see what
> it means to go on a branding tour around the

country and help people with their messaging, right?

Michelle was aware of how she felt when she was in creation mode. She was aware this mode would lead her to her purpose. She knew this. She knew what made her feel expansive. It's so hard to break away from typical expectations if you don't truly know your own quirks and all; keep this idea in your pocket because we'll be getting quirky later when you learn how to play with your imagination from a former CMO.

Loss for you may be the realization that the person you are now is not who you used to be, and you want to change. You may have lost the old you when you became a mom and the challenges of parenthood have forced you to adapt in ways you didn't want to or plan to. Looking at/processing/working through that loss is hard. You may be fearful of taking the next step, but if you're prepared to face that fear I'm going to show you some ways to do that.

When Michelle explained her method of challenging expectations by picking the skills she wanted to build and fears she wanted to face she emphasized that you must pick a real weakness not a fake one.

In her words:

> I love really switching or flipping the script on
> life that way. I find that empowering. I find
> that really scary, though, like really, really scary,
> when you really think about it. We could always
> rationalize ourselves and dilute our problems and
> be like, yeah, I'm kind of sort of afraid of public
> speaking. So let me go to Toastmasters and, in
> reality—you're really, really scared of something
> much bigger.

Michelle is referring to the weaknesses that might bring
you to your knees. I think this is a key distinction because
it strips us from glossing over our deepest fears. Michelle's
journey gives us an introduction into many of the things
we will cover in my book, the importance of fearlessly
embracing the challenge of changing your life script, taking
control of your own destiny, connecting with a supportive
community, and trusting yourself. Your imagination can
help you find ways to chart a new course.

When I climbed the Sydney Harbor Bridge I wanted
to feel what it was like to stare down my fear and celebrate
in the euphoria of not letting it beat me or stop me. Years
later I was looking down into the blue ocean from a small
plane over the Whitsundays on the way to the Great Barrier

Reef. I was holding my breath until we landed, but I was able to be present. Earlier in my life I'd get on a roller coaster with my eyes closed. Today I might keep my eyes open. It has changed the way my kids see me. They had been nervous about my bridge climb but now they see it as part of who I am and how I roll. I wanted to be able to draw on that feeling of accomplishment whenever I was confronted by a fear in the future. My climb may not have been a historical moment worthy of a textbook mention but it changed me. I saw that I could walk across a bridge and not freeze like a helpless bird. It's now important for you to consider the last time you felt powerful. When was the last time you were brave? That brave woman is still inside of you. It's time to reexamine what we think we need to be powerful and make an impact. Let's see how coming from a humble environment or lacking resources today doesn't have to make you feel powerless. This next podcast guest inspired me to rethink how I was using my power. I want to remind you that you can reawaken your imagination and find the proof you need to act like the powerhouse that you actually are. Want to reclaim your power? Let's go!

Your turn to take what you've learned in this chapter to reawaken your imagination. Use the following section to tailor the lessons you've uncovered from this chapter to fuel your imagination this week.

BIG IDEAS

- Practice facing your fears on your own terms so that you can strengthen those muscles when things are outside of your control
- Don't be a dweeb. Pick honest fears to confront.
- Use your imagination to tailor this approach based on your budget
- Next time the world expects you to recoil, consider stepping forward

IMAGINATION WARM-UPS

1. In what two or three situations have you feared going off script; not doing what was expected as a daughter, sister, or mom? What was really behind those fears?

2. Think about now: what is your biggest fear these days that you'd want to work through so that when new situations pop up you'll be more prepared to face and perhaps make unexpected choices that work better for you?

3. Imagine some "really close to it" ways you can face this fear during this year.

4. Imagine the kind of person you want to be when you've faced this fear. I am the kind of person who can now....

5. How would you want your kids to see you in relation to how you work through challenges?

Chapter 5

RECLAIM YOUR POWER

-MUYAMBI MUYAMBI, THE FOUNDER OF CYCLE CONNECT

In this chapter you will:

- Discuss how power, confidence, self-trust, and energy are all important in anything that you do
- Be reminded that you **are** capable of more
- Recognize how you are already using your power, as a mom, to shape the next generation
- Question why you aren't using your power to achieve your personal goals
- Realize that it takes knowing how to reclaim your power when you need it

SOMETIMES YOU NEED to be reminded of how powerful you truly are. I've heard it's hard for some moms to imagine themselves as powerful, but we've all had those moments when we astounded ourselves. When was yours? How long ago was it? I've felt powerless more often than powerful. Many of the moms I know would agree with that statement. How about you? Perhaps it's when someone won't listen to your advice? Maybe you see an injustice but feel you don't have the power to intervene and make a difference? Or maybe it's when someone is telling you what you want is wrong. When you think about it, women (in general) can create and live a life at the same time. Wow! That's pretty amazing. Why don't women claim their power? Why aren't we walking around feeling ten feet tall? It should make more of us feel powerful! Let me give you an example of when I felt powerless and had to reclaim my ability to impact change in my own life.

Math has never been my strong suit, yet there I was taking an entrance exam for business school and my analytical skills were on the line. I had spent months studying for the GMAT; obsessing about getting a graduate degree and ensuring I could qualify for grants to pay for it. The day of my exam the pressure had mounted so much that I went brain dead in the math section. I stopped trying midway. It's like my ability to come up with creative problem-solving solutions was totally offline. I bombed the GMAT. That moment was one where I felt powerless. If someone had sat right next to me and grabbed my hand to select answers, even they wouldn't have been able to make me do it.

Nevertheless I decided to try again and the next thirty days were nothing short of a math miracle. I laser-focused only on the math section of the GMAT. I had to forget that during elementary school I buckled under pressure and gave up on every Math Bee preparation. When we'd go up in front of the class and have to answer math equations my brain was SO deathly afraid of being embarrassed that I never even tried. I'd just blurt out an answer to get out of what looked like a firing squad of faces looking back at me.

Now I had to teach myself the math skills I had never learned. Math anxieties could no longer play a role, not this time. So when I took the test again thirty days later the second I caught myself freaking out I had to shut up that familiar doubting voice and tap into a power I didn't know I had. I boosted my score 200 miraculous points; this was huge and opened the door to an Ivy League business school filled with geniuses. If I can be in the same place as former engineers and hedge fund managers, then I must have done something really right.

When I feel powerless I think about that GMAT and I like to recall another time when I felt the magnitude of my power. On my firstborn's second birthday I took a pregnancy test and it was positive. Six weeks in I was so nauseated that I told my husband jokingly [*God, I was only joking!*]: "This better be twins, because I am more nauseous than the first time around." You know those nausea-fixing bracelets out there? I was wearing two sets at one point, because it turned out I was right, it was twins. This pregnancy would, however, lead me to an incredibly powerful experience.

After I had successfully delivered my first twin, everyone around me, including a group of medical students, was freaking out because sometimes the birth of the second twin requires a C-section. Somehow I knew Nick, the second twin, would be out in no time. It was in those nine minutes between the birth of my two sons that I felt the true magnitude of my power. I felt as if I had an insider's perspective that no one on the outside could possibly have. I used this ability to imagine myself communicating with Nick, it was time for him to stop dilly-dallying and join Noah. I was conjuring my power and coaching Nick to conjure his. Sure enough, he did.

At the end of that day I was in pain, yes, but I grabbed onto a sense of peace. I am so grateful for the experience because so few moms have that opportunity. It is an experience I reflect on when I want to connect my imagination to what I am truly capable of.

This brings me to a podcast guest who used an experience of powerlessness to claim his power. When he was a freshman in college he decided to create a nonprofit that still continues to solve the transportation needs of villages in Africa today; meet Muyambi.

Muyambi was born in a remote village in Uganda. As a child, he almost died when he was seriously ill and the nearest hospital was a long way from his home. He would have died from malaria but a neighbor, who had a bicycle, took him to the hospital. In a remote African village if you needed to go to the hospital the choice was to be carried by your brothers or to borrow a neighbor's bicycle (if it was really serious). So many of us witness others' difficulties, yet few of us ask ourselves: what can I really do to help? Muyambi found a way, later in life, to do something about his childhood experience. When Muyambi was a freshman at Bucknell University, in Pennsylvania, he shared the story of how he founded Cycle Connect. I was astounded. You may think because Muyambi was a millennial college kid he had delusionally high hopes of changing the world. I want to stop you right there. Muyambi could have come up with a long list of reasons why he couldn't try to solve this challenge. He was far away from Uganda, a student without means, new to the U.S., alone, overwhelmed, and had no connections. Yet he used his power. People were attracted to him because they aligned with his values and the vision he was able to communicate.

He did not have one of those out-of-sight, out-of-mind moments when he left Uganda for college in Pennsylvania. Instead, Muyambi had the experience of a deeply personal problem many Ugandans face, and he recognized when he had the power to do something about it.

This is what Muyambi shared about the value of transportation in any remote village around the world.

In Uganda, a bicycle means a lot. I have so many stories of people who have been in the situation where a child needs to get to the hospital in the middle of the night. They may have to be carried there, and you don't know if you'll get them there in time. There is also the pressure of choosing what to use your money for, right? One critical aspect is transportation; yet there are others. So do you rent a motorcycle to get that child to the hospital but then not have the money to pay for the medical bills? Or do you walk with the child to the hospital but not get them there in time even though you have the money to pay the medical bills? So there are so many decisions that are buried within that challenge of transportation that not so many people have to think about here in the U.S., right?

As moms, we are well aware of decision fatigue. Imagine if this level of life-or-death decision-making was added to your day. It's easy to look away from that reality, for a myriad of reasons. We may think: *Someone must be handling that, right? Surely we can't be living in a world where these issues are being ignored?* It's easy to be distracted by our own lives. When you see images of poverty on TV it's easy to think they look fabricated. Even if you do care and see them as real, many of us don't take steps to help. Why is that?

In my opinion, Muyambi was motivated into action because he didn't need anyone but himself to use his power. He used what he had at the time. He was ready to go down his path alone if no one was willing to help him. You and I can learn from Muyambi—despite our differences. You too can use your power without needing anyone to tap you on the shoulder. Muyambi could have been distracted, consumed by his lack of experience, overwhelmed by an unfamiliar culture and zero budget. Ultimately, you have power and you get to choose, like Muyambi, whether to use it or not.

He also didn't waste time questioning whether he could make a big enough impact. He wasn't worried about the fact that he was just a college student. Instead, Muyambi decided to focus on refining his vision. He saw the challenge and rather than close his eyes he put a magnifying glass on the challenge. Then he sold his vision and shared his perspective with his social justice classmates and earned a grant from the Clinton Global Initiative, a Clinton Foundation program. For Muyambi, his early childhood experiences provided powerful moments that made an impression on his heart.

There's a lot to unpack here about having power and how to use it to the fullest extent. In a nutshell, you may be more capable than you give yourself credit for. I have heard many reasons why some of my clients think they can't or shouldn't step into their greatness. We might use our kids as our excuse. In reality it's never them, it's always us. **As a mom you have a unique perspective, love, and reason to feel powerful.** Let's go back to the script we have been handed as moms. We have power.

Muyambi's power was in his ability to see the impact bicycles could have on the lives of the people in remote villages. He could also communicate this vision to his peers who wanted to make a difference in the world. He held onto the memory that as a kid with malaria he was powerless to do anything; it was a feeling he didn't forget.

We went from distributing 100 bikes, every so often, whenever I could go home, to doing 2,000 bicycles a year. Now we are reaching over 6,000 families and 40,000 people. We've been able to skyrocket from a student organization to a full-fledged organization. It is serving a lot of people in

providing products that are way beyond bikes, now
we do oxen, motorcycles, grinding machines, pretty
much all productive assets that are provided to
farmers and taking them out of the cycle of poverty.

Don't focus on the obstacles, think about times where you
felt powerful; draw on that feeling. Use your imagination to
see the change you can make if you use your power. You have
power. Are you a strong communicator? Do your friends ask
you for insights on how to approach challenges? Do you have
something you can do that is powerful? Look for it and use
what you have. It's useful to engage your imagination when
answering these questions. It is through that lens that you
can decide to put a magnifying glass on a challenge that you
want to solve in your lifetime. Are you like Muyambi? You
once felt powerless but you have found the power within.
There is power in being a mom, you are responsible for guid-
ing your kids on their future path, you are their role model
and teacher.

You are powerful. Use that power by stepping into
the arena. **You are not meant to just stand on the sidelines.**
You can rewrite that part of the script you may have been
handed. Use your imagination. Again, in our youth, many
of us have been braver in using whatever power we thought
we had. So what about you, a mom in your thirties, forties,
or fifties? You know better or at least you think you should.

Let's learn about someone who has been through a lot of life, suffered bankruptcies, and managed to retain a good relationship with her now-adult kids after pursuing plant medicine and spiritually healing experiences that brought her to the jungle plenty of times—and a sometimes stinky entrepreneurial adventure!

Your turn to take what you've learned in this chapter to reawaken your imagination. Use the following section to tailor the lessons you've uncovered from this chapter to fuel your imagination this week.

BIG IDEAS

- You always have power; whether you choose to use it is up to you
- Focus on what you have and that alone is enough to get started
- Don't assume anyone else is handling it
- Take the time to remind yourself of when you felt most powerful on a weekly basis
- Deciding to become a mom is a powerful choice and so was picking up this book. Keep reading. You will find the right insights you can apply to your life. Stretch your imagination, find your superpower; own it

IMAGINATION WARM-UPS

1. When have you felt powerless? Imagine rewriting that narrative to regain your power.

2. As a little girl, when did you feel most powerful?

3. When have you felt most powerful in recent memory? Record that image in your mind for use whenever you need it.

4. What gifts are you best known for today?

5. What challenges can you imagine fixing if you felt powerful enough?

Chapter 6

BUILD YOUR SELF-TRUST

-SUZY BATIZ, THE INVENTOR OF POO~POURRI

In this chapter, you will:

- Learn about self-trust and how essential it is to make a change in your life
- Explore and start to heal your relationship with feeling like a "creative person"
- Earn your trust and believe you will know what's right for you
- Rethink why we struggle, so you won't waste your energy
- Stretch your thinking about who you are

BEING CONSIDERED CREATIVE has always been important to me. Sometimes the words "imagination" and "creativity" are used interchangeably; you need your imagination to think of new ideas, and the process of doing so is being creative. It can apply to a new business idea as much as it can to creating art. Do you consider yourself to be creative? Does this adjective fit like a glove? Has anyone ever called you creative? Alternatively, has anyone ever considered you entrepreneurial? Full of business ideas? In my life, using my imagination has been an emotional journey. Sometimes I didn't tell anyone about my ideas because I didn't want to be judged. Whether someone agrees that you are creative is subjective. I also didn't want my creations to be judged. If I started to call myself creative then how was I going to keep up that reputation? What if people disagreed about whether my creations were creative? Would I need to constantly come up with good ideas on the fly? It felt like a lot of pressure. But secretly, I've always yearned to be seen as creative.

Growing up I gleaned from others' reactions that I wasn't creative. If I sang at home I was told I was out of tune. When I danced I was laughed at for not having the Puerto Rican rhythm that I was supposed to have. At school, classmates were celebrated for their creativity especially when it came to artsy science projects. Later on, my writing needed a lot of help all through college. I must have been the most frequent visitor at NYU's Writing Workshop.

All of my papers were redlined by someone in that office. I had a lot to say. However, I had a lot to heal before I could find the courage to say things in a way that would be really understood by others. It was hard to complete my thoughts. I needed to challenge the voices from my past that told me I was not very creative.

Think about your past. Was there someone who put down your ideas? Use your imagination to remember the moments when you started to doubt your ability to be imaginative/creative. You need to process how you feel about being imaginative.

If you are going to learn how to reawaken your imagination and trust yourself, it's important to address how you feel about it. **Anyone who has a business idea will need a solid and reliable relationship with being imaginative and creative.**

As a kid, I remember wanting to launch my own business. I was serious; I took out a green-covered book about becoming entrepreneurial from the library. I wanted to see if I could find an idea, any idea, for a business that would fit into my life. This was before the Internet. Some ideas included being a dog walker or mowing someone's lawn. (These ideas stand out in my memory because I didn't see myself doing them. I lived in a concrete jungle and was afraid of dogs.) Back then, it felt like those opportunities to make money were something only boys did. Delivering newspapers was another ridiculous option for a girl who'd never learned to ride a bike. Those options in that book felt uninspiring or unsafe. The only one I did try was babysitting. This attempt to be entrepreneurial was hindered by the fact that I was a child of divorced parents and lived between their two households. I only spent some weekends with my dad in the suburbs where the work was, so my income was capped. Back then, I was desperate to be entrepreneurial, and earn more than what a few Saturday nights' worth of childcare would pay. However, behind the scenes, I was deeply insecure. I didn't think I had the ability to be an entrepreneur. More importantly I doubted anyone thought my skills were worth paying for. Creating a business felt incredibly scary and frankly dangerous as a little girl, so I shelved that green-covered book for decades.

Given my past you can see that deciding to launch my own business has forced me to confront all these demons and grow up emotionally. You may be interested in using your reawakened imagination to launch a business. But to do so, and weather all the entrepreneurial storms that exist, it's necessary to do the inner work. A podcast guest who has done a great deal of self-reflection and adjusted her approach to both building a business and living her life is Suzy Batiz, the founder and inventor of several products/brands including Poo~Pourri and supernatural. Suzy is intimately familiar with such storms and she's gained massive wisdom for us all.

I have admired Suzy for years. She is a mom and grandmother who is also on the *Forbes* list of America's eighty richest self-made women. I admire her most for learning to trust herself. Suzy has survived two bankruptcies and has spoken about how humiliating it was to tell her family that she was bankrupt. She has taken some radical steps to develop her trust in herself as a businesswoman and as a mother. These steps have included trips to the South American jungle to experience the spiritual benefits of psychedelics to heal from childhood traumas. As a mom she also had to feel at peace with the fact she had raised a son who could also trust himself without her. This self-trust was tested when Suzy's son headed to the jungle on his own to use ayahuasca. When was the last time you trusted yourself? Personally, I'm still in the shaky-ground stage. I too easily turn to Google or other moms for wisdom, which I actually already have. In my experience, if I had only trusted myself, I could have spared myself many tears and avoided feeling anxious about events that often turned out to be NOTHING! Can you relate? We shall see how things progress. My sons are only eight and eleven, so I have a few years ahead.

When I got the opportunity to interview Suzy, I needed to be really organized (it was 2 a.m. in Sydney, where I was living). I didn't know if I could trust myself enough to think on my feet at that time of the morning. So, I made sure to draft clear questions that I could read, if necessary, rather than rely on my usual improvisational style. It turned out that this extra care was a good thing. Suzy told me how refreshing and fun it was sitting with my questions. I used my imagination to brainstorm deep and thought-provoking questions because I wanted Suzy to see my sincerity and to feel like she had new things to share with my listeners.

She helped me make sense of my own ways of expressing myself. This is why I know that by applying her insights you will have a starting place to feel secure or to trust yourself enough to use your imagination and express your creativity. You will read later about Sundance Film Festival winner Diane Bell and how sometimes you'll need to trust yourself more than experts if you want to pursue some big dreams. You'll be able to imagine more because you will have decluttered any bad thoughts from your head and let in more thoughts from the infinite universe. Many of my podcast guests believe the universe is where often the best ideas come from.

It is important you feel good about reawakening your imagination, not bad or hesitant based on what someone told you back in fifth grade. Be aware of how the most innocuous comment can derail your self-trust.

Suzy shared how a comment from her son set off a sense of fear.

> I had just written a sitcom that we were pitching. And my agent was like, "Would you act in it?" My son was on the call and he says, "Have you seen her in front of a camera?" I immediately felt this fear and I was like, whoa, okay. What's that? That's very similar to jumping off a cliff. Like, what? Why would I act? And I don't know.
>
> I felt scared. So let me take some acting lessons and see what that feels like within me, but it's not because of trauma, it's because I want to see if I can do it. And that's where the courage, I think, comes in.

You know that whatever you put out there will be judged. Our parents judge us. Strangers do too, especially if you put yourself out there on the Internet and social media. We have a choice; to succumb or resist it. Everything starts with acceptance of that judgment. You want to be creative? Acknowledge that every creator before you has had their critics too. Don't waste your finite energy fighting it. Why not reserve your energy to produce your best life's work instead? Struggling is part of our shared human experience.

There is a feeling of peace that comes with accepting the struggle to be imaginative and sharing your creations and ideas with people.

Suzy can appreciate life as it is, she says:

> To think that we're not going to struggle is absolute insanity because every single person has struggled. So if it wasn't part of our evolutionary human plan, why would everybody struggle or suffer?

> It's just part of it. So instead of thinking, "I shouldn't struggle" or "I shouldn't suffer," it's like, "How can I build my own internal well-being?" It's like floating down a river. How can I be the water? As opposed to, you know, I struggled, it shouldn't have happened, it shouldn't have happened. I'm like, Oh, that is so "victim mentality." How can I be like, "You know what? I saw that rock ahead and I didn't move to the left, you know, next time I'm going to move to the left." Okay.

Once you accept that using your imagination may trigger other people to criticize you then you can figure out how to navigate that reality and learn from the process. **You have**

to trust that what you offer is of value. The main lesson that Suzy provides is about learning how to trust yourself. Suzy says that rather than expecting validation from other people, why not build your ability to trust yourself?

Suzy has a transformational online program called Alive OS® where she helps participants rebuild their inner trust.

Suzy says this about one lesson from this program:

> One thing I do is to go back and have participants harvest from their failures. I take people back to the point of when they knew not to do something because you generally always know. There's always a point where you're like, "Oh, I remember that feeling. I remember going, no, don't do that. But I did it anyway."

> I removed myself from being a victim. "Oh, shit. I knew that I shouldn't have done that. Right. I knew it. And I did it anyway." That's where I can start trusting myself because when I'm doing it, I'm being accountable. I'm like, "You knew, Suzy, you knew. Okay, next time let's see if we can close that gap."

That gap closes with experience. You must earn your own trust to close that gap. It takes practice. In your case, you may need to share your ideas with more people. Baby steps. Then accept the critics will emerge, and respond if you need to. See if you can trust yourself to do so gracefully. Breathe before you react. This way rather than feeling hesitant to be creative because of other people's opinions, you will remember that you can't please everyone and when you don't you will know what to say. Do this enough times and then you will feel less hesitant about calling yourself imaginative or creative and you won't need to wait for someone to validate you.

The benefit of clearing out old thoughts about whether you are creative will be worth it for this adventure of learning how to reawaken your imagination. You need to make peace with how the world might react to the results of your imagination. If you are not at peace about being judged and you don't trust that you will be able to handle critics or be resilient then I can't blame you for being hesitant to share what's in your imagination with the world or anyone else. You will feel blocked. If you are scared, you won't be open to all the creative ideas your imagination can generate.

Suzy shared how during this pandemic so many people were terrified. It had taken a lot of inner work for her to learn how not to be terrified too. As a business owner she needed to be creative about her offerings during the pandemic to survive. She needed to keep her pipeline to her imagination open; how else would she have been able to adjust her business?

This is how Suzy puts it:

> So when I'm so terrified anytime somebody says boo, how am I going to be still? Right? So I'm reacting. I'm like, "Oh, I'm going to try to let infinite wisdom come in there." You know, it's not going to come in. So let me deal with my own terror and deal with my own pain first. Then infinite wisdom is a natural state of being, I don't have to concentrate on letting it in, because that pipeline is just more open.

This is the foundation to exploring your imagination. You will need to clear up how you feel about being creative or innovative, and then things can come together with greater ease. It's important to also be practical about the reality of putting your heart out there. You will be judged. The key is to be able to rely on yourself that you will know what to do when you hear critics. This trust is earned and 100 percent within your control. This works whether you love thinking about yourself as creative or feel self-conscious about it, as I once did and as many of my clients do. Going through this works also as a parent, if you wish to teach your kids how to protect and nurture their imaginations. This requires healing the parts of you telling you that you're not creative, and then you can go wild! Consider your relationship to the idea that you are creative, and trust yourself enough to start thinking that you can be if you so choose. What if you thought of yourself as creative? What new decisions would you make? A lot of us suffer from decision fatigue; irrespective of your creative outlets, whether it's launching a business or picking a medium for your art, there are a lot of choices you must make once you use your imagination If you've ever wanted a shorthand for making all sorts of decisions, read the next chapter—I have enlisted the help of Michelle Florendo, a brilliant decision engineer from Stanford University with an unexpected perspective on the validity of making decisions using the somatic intelligence we all have within us.

Your turn to take what you've learned in this chapter to reawaken your imagination. Use the following section to tailor the lessons you've uncovered from this chapter to fuel your imagination this week.

BIG IDEAS

- You get to call yourself creative and act in alignment
- Take steps to earn self-trust and be intentional about this
- Practice being like water and float around struggles
- Accept ownership for the part you've played in situations to truly evolve

IMAGINATION WARM-UPS

1. Can you imagine three or four times when you doubted that you were creative? What if you hadn't doubted yourself?

2. When have you been the most creative or imaginative in your life? Write about your one favorite moment.

3. Where is your level of self-trust today? Imagine your self-trust in the context of putting yourself out there in person or online (do this on a scale from zero to ten, ten being totally trusting of yourself).

4. If you start doing small acts every day to build your self-trust, how can you imagine holding yourself accountable? Any habits you want to begin?

5. Think back to when you received criticism. Can you imagine how you could have handled it better, based on Suzy's guidance?

Chapter 7

MAKE DECISIONS WITH YOUR MULTIPLE CENTERS OF INTELLIGENCE

-MICHELLE FLORENDO, A STANFORD-TRAINED DECISION ENGINEER

In this chapter you will:

- Explore how to avoid decision fatigue
- Learn to feel more confident making a series of micro and macro decisions
- Be reminded that you can follow your gut instinct—your logical thinking brain is not the only rodeo in town
- Learn a framework you can use to feel more grounded and be more decisive

FINDING A BETTER WAY is valuable. For big decisions, like where to send our kids to school (or whether to send them to school) or whether to leave a career altogether, finding a better way can be invaluable. As part of my relocation adventures, there were so many decisions. Sometimes I broke like cheap lawn furniture trying to figure out every single next right step. Take picking a school for my three sons when I hadn't even visited the town where we were going to live on our return to the U.S., in Austin, Texas. My logical thinking drove me to open twenty-plus Internet tabs to compare and contrast schools, with top marks, in the area. If you overlay the schools in each school district with the driving distances to the center of the city and then take into account whether the properties have HVAC, you'll drive yourself nuts. Now, if I could just have trusted my gut and picked a place based on written school reviews and emailed the schools that sounded like safe and nurturing environments, I could have toggled between four tabs instead. Once I felt decision fatigue over those twenty-plus Internet tabs I reminded myself about how I'd mistakenly landed on my kids' school in Australia at the very last minute.

It's no wonder we feel decision fatigue; there are so many risks involved. If our decisions were made in isolation, making them might feel simpler and more within our control. But we don't live in a vacuum. Have your sound choices ever turned into flops? Anyone else buy a house at the top of the market like I did? So much energy is poured into making "good decisions," but what if there were a better and equally valid way?

Our gut could hold the answer. It comes in handy for decisions whether you're a career mom or not. The same thinking that might sound corporate here can be used to run a household or pick your kids' school. Soon you'll see that there are three phases to decision-making, and you will want to include your gut to meet them.

Have you ever had a gut feeling that you were out of alignment with what you were really meant to be doing? Over the past ten years, many of my corporate clients have experienced a variety of emotional ups and downs. Sometimes they wished they could feel as fulfilled as I did. When the pandemic rolled around, I spent more time convincing prospective clients about the attraction of a stable, full-time job than I did on selling my services. Something wasn't feeling right in my gut. Things were different and something needed to change.

What if I told you that your gut instinct is just as valid a source of information as your logical brain? What if Michelle Florendo, a Stanford-trained decision engineer, told you that? She did during our interview. Michelle also reminded me that there are multiple centers of intelligence—along with the gut and head, you have a heart.

You'll have a chance later in this book to see what can happen when you use your heart to make decisions. At this time, let's just wake up your imagination by using your gut and head. Going with your gut takes less energy than creating all those financial models. Often this logical thought processing is programmed into us. We have been sold the idea that logic trumps instincts. How we were raised affects how we make our decisions. **It turns out, some of us are making it hard for ourselves and wasting a lot of energy in our decision-making process.** What is your relationship with decisions? Michelle shared her thinking on this subject. First, have you ever beaten yourself up for having made a bad decision? I have and so did Michelle before she built her own independent practice.

In Michelle's words:

> I landed in consulting, which was fine, it was really interesting and fun for maybe about a year. Then I realized this was not something I wanted to do for the rest of my career. I remember feeling really lost. Maybe even more than feeling lost, I felt guilty and ashamed. I felt guilty for not being happy in this job that from the outside looked really great. Like who am I to be unhappy with my great job that other people would love to have?

> I also felt a bit of shame for thinking, "gosh, did I make a mistake?" Did I not know what I wanted? Had I made the wrong decision to go down this path? For a while, because I was feeling lost and ashamed and didn't want to admit to anyone that I had made a mistake, I didn't know what to do next.

In my ten years of coaching, this is why so many of my clients kept returning to corporate jobs or stayed put in bad situations. Many clients decided having an MBA was the best way to mitigate the risk of being unemployable sometime in their life. We didn't all pursue graduate degrees for our parents. But some did.

Some of my clients are only in their corporate careers because it's logical for them to be there. The money is good. That's what MBAs do. Anything else would be risky. I've been told by two clients who are obsessed with fitness: "You don't get a Harvard MBA to run a fitness gym." So they would never consider doing so. What about moms? Do you want to do something different, but there's something logical holding you back? Maybe you can't seem to make the first decision to make it happen.

Michelle recalls her teacher's framework for making a decision:

Professor Ron Howard would teach us about decisions. There are basically three components to any decision.

1. What are the objectives?
2. What are the options?
3. What information do you have on how each option might deliver against your objectives?

I think at that point in time I realized I had lived life according to objectives that were given to me; from my parents, from society, from all the other people that I went to school with. The first thing I needed to do was understand—when I peel back the layers of the onion, what is it that I actually want?

What do you really want? To really drill down for the answer, start by writing out what your parents would want you to want. Imagine an onion. Your parents' expectations is one layer you'll want to peel off. Then write out what society expects you to want. What if this layer were pulled off? Think about the people in your life, including any partners, peers, friends, moms, grandparents, etc. Look at what they would want you to want for yourself right now. Remove those layers. What are you left with?

Trust your gut; does this feel right?

If making decisions were a sterile practice, removing these layers would be an easy exercise. But it's just not. Some of us have been told we suck at making decisions. Others of us have been penalized by loved ones for making some decisions. Both situations are real to me. This might be where you need a third party to walk you through a similar process.

The next step is to write out what you are thinking. You can draw a decision tree or analyze numbers in Microsoft Excel. If you've been taught to use logical thinking to solve challenges, then start there. Michelle points to some traps that can keep someone in analysis paralysis. We have the tendency to overthink a lot of decisions—choices we might make more easily in calm environments but become like kryptonite in volatile and uncertain ones.

Remember those twenty tabs I had open when choosing a new school? Had I been making things needless-ly hard on myself all these years? Who knew using my logical brain took so much energy to make decisions? I could have made decisions more quickly by following my gut.

Michelle says this:

> That type of thinking, the maximizer mindset of, I don't want to make a decision until I absolutely know this decision is the best, is a trap. Instead, ask yourself: can you make a decision that is good enough? I know, depending on what culture you grew up in, how "good enough" might sound [like a low bar]. I don't want to settle for good. But again, what is more important, the pursuit of happiness or actually being happy? That's where being clear about what your objectives are and being able to define them with enough specificity to say when you've met them, is useful. The other trap that I think people fall into is thinking that this one decision is going to change the rest of my life. Whereas it's not actually that way. Life is the sum of all of these decisions that we make over time.

To reinforce this point, when it came to my Australian school-choosing process, I tried the tab thing, but timing forced my hand. I even spoke with the wrong school administrator before quickly Googling my only Montessori option. I had to trust a place that would feature both its good and bad reviews of the school, and in the end I went with my gut. Out of that relocation, I'm happy to report that my sons would have hated any school I enrolled them in. So whether I'd used my head or gut, the verdict would have been the same: anxiety-ridden, bloodbath-worthy morning struggles to get them out the door whether we were in the U.S. or Australia.

So far, with our return to America, I did email the two schools where we are enrolling our boys and the administrators sounded as warm and nurturing as I had hoped. Reassuringly, when I mistakenly told her the wrong birthdate for my twins, a school principal said, "We are all struggling with cognitive overload!"

Once you use your logical brain and come up with a good enough answer, then it's time to set your logical brain aside. This is where your intuition or gut has to take over. We are moms. I'm not going to pretend that we have infinite sources of energy (however if you read the James Altucher chapter then you'll know you can always find some more!). I suffer from decision fatigue all of the time. In 2022, I decided to write a book, and every letter of every word in it is a decision. We are all yearning for shortcuts. The sad state of affairs is, our intuition has long been pooh-poohed as a smart way to approach decision-making. We can fill a whole book on why.

Michelle explains this further:

> Our lived experiences are embedded in our so-
> matic intelligence. That's the gut. There's a rea-
> son why when we face a decision, we may have
> a gut feeling. It's very quick. It's hard for us to
> articulate because that intelligence is coming up
> so quickly and is often quicker than our brain can
> process. But it is coming from somewhere. It's of-
> ten coming from the amalgamation or combina-
> tion of everything that we've experienced. And
> so being able to make more intuitive, less effort-
> ful decisions is actually reconnecting to those
> other pieces of intelligence that we have. So how
> is it that we can use these emotions as data? How
> is it that we can use these gut feelings as data and
> become more acclimated to understanding where
> they're coming from and what they're trying to
> tell us?

So what is that decision you must make? Apply your logical
thinking methods to make a decision. Then ask yourself a
series of questions to see how you feel about the decision
that you came up with, using your logical brain.

Michelle provides this example:

If you're choosing between two things, let's say to the right, you have Choice A. To the left, you have Choice B. Imagine stepping into Choice A on the right, and tune into what feelings come up, what emotions. Also how does that feel in your body?

Ask yourself: is what I'm feeling consistent or contrary to what my brain is saying?

If it's contrary, then that becomes an opportunity to dig deeper. What am I feeling? Is it fear? What is the fear of? Is it fear of uncertainty? Is it fear of something different? And is that necessarily bad? Like what is that emotion telling me?

Tune into your bodily sensation. Do you feel tension and constriction? Or do you feel a settling and a centeredness? What happens to your heart rate as you think about going a certain direction versus the other? Give yourself space to explore. What's coming up? Where's it coming from? What is it telling me? How might I use this as data?

We need more than logical thinking to make decisions en route to becoming great. All our wisdom and emotional intelligence is needed today to change the scope of what's possible. You're it. We're it. So what decision are you contemplating that once decided can help you step into your greatness?

Your turn to take what you've learned in this chapter to reawaken your imagination. Use the following section to tailor the lessons you've uncovered from this chapter to fuel your imagination this week.

BIG IDEAS

- Your gut instinct can get you to an answer faster
- Go for good enough decision-making
- Don't beat yourself up if you get it wrong; there are outside factors always at play
- Somatic experiences are data too

IMAGINATION WARM-UPS

1. What decisions are you most proud of? Imagine yourself back then. What feelings came up for you upon reflecting on those moments?

2. Can you imagine having a better relationship with making decisions? An even more positive one if that's already your starting place? How might that look?

3. Think about an important decision you'd like to make within the next month. What would your objective be? What information do you have as it relates to going with one choice over another? Imagine how picking one option would theoretically play out and then the other options too. Which options can you cross off?

4. Are you ready to take your thinking cap off now? Do it! Imagine picking the best choice in front of you. What feelings pop up for what that might mean in the greater context of your life?

5. What's the best choice today based on having done that exercise? Imagine being at peace with yourself even if something outside of your

control makes that decision not achieve your desired outcome. For example, if you buy a house in an area with projected housing appreciation costs and the housing market falls in two years... this wouldn't mean your initial decision-making process was wrong. You are not a genie.

Chapter 8

ENERGIZE YOUR DREAMS

-JAMES ALTUCHER, THE AUTHOR OF *CHOOSE YOURSELF*

In this chapter you will:

- Understand the importance of creating the energy you will need to pursue a big dream

- Discover why feeling drained is not something you have to live with

- Learn you may need more energy than you think

- Examine emotional energy vampires, which as a mom, you will need to be mindful of

- Explore a framework to create more energy for yourself

WORKING MOMS CLOCK a lot of shifts: the morning fiasco as we get our kids ready for school; our paid jobs, which last all day; and then feeding the family in the evening before finally opening our laptops when the kids are in bed to tie up loose ends. Stay-at-home moms, especially if they once worked, bring the same draining fast pace and high expectations into their homes. For them it may be perfectly folded laundry and Pinterest-worthy family-photo sessions. Ultimately, I don't see very many fresh-eyed and bushy-tailed moms around me. Stay tuned because I interviewed Jo Dodd, who is a mom, and I will share her story of how keeping ourselves busy is more of a mindset than an actual job hazard. So ultimately the question on your mind is probably this: who the hell has the energy to pursue dreams? And if you feel low on energy right now, then what levers can you pull to raise it?

Landing several guests on my podcast did consume an enormous amount of energy. Getting the attention of Gary Vaynerchuk (GaryVee) and James Altucher, with their millions of followers, required me to practically bust at my seams to be heard in an ultra-competitive sea. However, putting myself on that quest energized me. We tend to forget this can happen. You might not have energy right now, but if you plug yourself into the right mission you may find yourself energized twofold. But first, let's talk about energy as a finite resource before you find what energizes you. James Altucher, the host of *The James Altucher Show* podcast, says this about energy:

> Every day you're allotted a certain amount of energy. You wake up, and it's already been given to you, the amount of energy you have for that day. Energy is the only way to succeed at anything. If you wake up and you're too tired for the day, then you'll go back to sleep and you'll accomplish nothing. If you wake up and you have a ton of energy, then you'll maybe accomplish a lot, do things [that require the energy]. For example, if you're reinventing yourself or trying to reach your peak potential, or trying to bounce back from failure, or trying to be successful in either a relationship or a career or a sport or an activity that you love you need a lot of energy.

Energy, that's something that many of us just don't have enough of. James says to be successful in an activity that you love, you need a lot of it. What's a modern mom to do? At some point, you need to choose yourself, which also happens to be the name of James Altucher's book.

Start by thinking about your current mom script and ask yourself if it's really what you want to do or if it's something you think you *should* do. You need to pursue what's in your heart, because going after what someone else wants for you is draining. Being someone that you are not is an energy vulture and a time sucker. In my case, I experienced a huge energy suck in my twenties by pursuing the wrong career, when I could have used that virgin energy to be successful in a career that I actually loved. At that time, I was using my energy to make my abuela proud.

My paternal grandmother told me to become a professional. If I had to define what she meant I'd say that she wanted me to go to an office building, in a skirt. She wanted me to get a college degree. It was her dream to see me filthy rich and independent. Her dream would have been for me to bring home the bacon, like my husband...then buy and also cook the bacon and every single night clean my entire house so there'd be no bacon grease on my pristine walls. I was supposed to do it all, in her eyes. This is the interpretation of the American Dream according to a Cuban woman who still lived like it was the Great Depression every day.

James Altucher once worked for HBO in a conventional role that would meet the specs for an American Dream type of job. Today he is a multi-millionaire, an author, an investor, and an incredible podcaster. It's important to note that James, early in his career, needed tons of energy too. During those early days he was working full-time for HBO while he was building his entrepreneurial ventures; he was also a dad. Imagine *that* grind! His sacrifices paid off, but then bankruptcies came his way. James talks about energy from the perspective of someone who built businesses and later needed the energy to get out from under their rubble to rebuild his wealth.

Guests on his show include professional poker players, comedians, and all sorts of dreamers turned doers. I think his career today is more interesting than his media one. I know a lot of media folks. Yet, I can't say I know a lot of fulfilled ones. This is why I admire James. In his work, he has made a distinction between the American Dream and an individual dream.

In James Altucher's words, here's the difference:

I think actual individual dreams are separate from the American Dream. All props to America, but individual dreams are often higher. You know, you say you want to be, when you're six years old, you want to be an astronaut, you want to be on the radio, which is what a podcast kind of is, you want to have a show, you want to create art, you want to write a book, strengthen your body and be an athlete. Those are individual dreams and not the American Dream.

My abuela didn't have the energy to chase her dreams. She had my dad at forty in the 1950s; she worked in factories as a seamstress. She rented out every square foot of her house. Sacrifice was her middle name. Her dreams were born out of necessity. James's idea of an individual dream would have been frivolous to Abuela. She didn't revisit her path toward amassing wealth because she was on a bullet train headed straight into retirement. She wasn't looking to build up a set of skills. She never sat in a classroom being told that she could one day lead a nation either. I was raised differently; I went to college and heard messages that I was special and talented.

In the middle of my first semester at law school I realized that becoming an attorney wasn't for me. I decided to rewrite my script; Abuela's version of the American dream wasn't mine. I finally saw, with my own eyes, how mechanical and assembly-lined this highly esteemed professional path had become. I also found my time at law school draining; I wasn't excited about legal topics at all. They didn't energize me. I could understand why my family thought it was a worthy pursuit, but this wasn't how I wanted to spend my life. Going for something just because the path was there, to prove I could do it, wasn't enough to make me jump out of bed.

So, I set out to uncover my individual dreams. Finding myself, or taking a gap year, wasn't condoned in my family. Nevertheless, I had the energy and an inquisitive nature and I did it anyway. I went on a quest to find a career that really interested me. Some people questioned my quest but others encouraged me, telling me one day the information I was gathering would be helpful. I carefully planned, cold-called, and asked lots of questions. Along the way I documented the insights I was learning. It was a project. I didn't have an income. My abuela would have vomited had this been her. I took the opportunity to ask nutritionists, advertising executives, marketers, guidance counselors, anyone who would answer my questions about their jobs.

If you are at home with your children, this is something that you can do. Reevaluate your dreams; are they enough, too much, or entirely wrong? I have coached many women who never stopped to reflect on their career choices. Time is the ultimate excuse. The reality is, it's more than time that stops us from taking a break and reflecting. It requires our energy, a precious resource to any mom. James gives us a clue about why energy is needed, if you decide to take a less conventional route. Frankly, when he describes what we might be up against, it could stop any tired mom in her tracks. But don't worry, pursuing the right ambitions can energize you too, which I'll speak more on later. You'll need energy not just to execute your ideas but also to confront the challenges that James mentions:

It's hard every year to reinvent yourself, because it's scary. To be the hero you have to fight the dragon. In a fairy tale, the hero defeats the dragon or the dragons, pretty scary. Most people who try to fight a dragon are going to die. And that's what it is to reinvent yourself, to reinvent a career—even though it might be worth it. You might be the hero, you might become the king, whatever your dream is. You also could get killed or damaged in some way, and there's usually a lot of damage associated with reinvention.

The best example I can share with you about trying and failing to find the courage to change is from before I became a mom. I had less confidence in my own ability before I pushed my three sons out. Many other moms also recall how low on self-esteem they were in their twenties.

After I finally quit law school I decided to pursue advertising, something I had considered decades earlier. So I began cold-calling ad agencies. I finally snagged a meeting with a copywriter in a small agency in Tribeca. It was my first break into the career I had decided was for me. I didn't know the copywriter, but this guy gave me a copywriting assignment anyway. I had to create taglines for a travel destination. Remember, I had been walking the streets of NYC for weeks, praying for this one opportunity to manifest itself. This was my shot. I returned home and I brainstormed and brainstormed. I knew I could come up with some sensational sentences...and then I didn't. I never returned to that copywriter with my taglines. I froze from all of the pressure I put on myself. I wished I could have known James Altucher back then. It seems my reaction is to be expected during a reinvention.

So here is what James Altucher says happens when you reinvent yourself:

> Everybody's got imperfections. Sometimes when you're reinventing yourself, it's the imperfections and the fears, and the blind spots we have about our strengths and weaknesses that suddenly flare up and try to bring us down or self-sabotage us. And it's really hard to survive that.

All of my fears flared up between the time I was handed that assignment and the moment I decided not to hand it in.

This is a hard story for me to tell, even today. I've written articles for many publications, but being a creative writer felt very different. Recall Suzy Batiz's take on trusting yourself and your creative decisions. My written word for, say, *Forbes* or Huffington Post, feels safe. Whereas calling myself a "creative" feels gigantic. It once felt like a title I couldn't carry—just yet. While it's been hard for me to make that leap, getting over it (and other things) has gotten easier after becoming a mom. **Anything is less embarrassing than farting in the delivery room in front of a male nurse.** Would you agree that some things that embarrassed you before being a mom wouldn't now?

Fast-forward decades later. I eventually did end up working in advertising but it was never in a role in the creative department, what I truly desired. This still was before becoming a mom. The creative department is the area for anyone who dares to think that they have a useful imagination. It takes audacity to be in that crew. My self-belief in my ability to get paid for my imagination was really low. Why was that? Because it was exactly what I wanted.

James is right. I saw my blind spots when I was making my rounds in those fancy advertising agencies. I came up against my weakness of fearing I wasn't creative enough and I would be found out if I handed in that assignment. It was a hard realization. I knew what worked to land a corporate job but to become a copywriter? I had no idea.

It was also a time when I had more energy to set off on a new path. I was a single woman on her own who had rent to pay. What you have at stake might be a little different. I wasn't a mom when I was slaying dragons. **However, I know moms can slay dragons—ask an NICU mom who had to battle months apart from her newborn or one who went** through rounds upon rounds of IVF treatments. Those who took a "sword" during a C-section are knightly too.

You might not have the energy to pursue your individual dream because your plate is too full today. Or you may not know how to begin. These things might be true, but you'll never know if you had it in you if you don't give your individual dream a chance. Hand in your copywriting assignment—don't do what I did.

Do this instead....

Be confident you can pursue your individual dream.

Next, let's use your imagination to add energy to your day, so that you can have it for the things that would bring you real joy.

It takes energy to walk a different path. It takes energy to stop the momentum of your current life. It takes a massive amount of energy to redirect your efforts in a new and uncertain direction. I bet you're wondering how you could possibly change direction when you're already exhausted? James focuses on four ways to get energy. He speaks about **eating, moving, sleeping**, and **emotional health**. This got me thinking: *I've heard this before. I have heard it for decades. Yet, I never tried focusing on all four at the same time.* If we are twinsies then perhaps you haven't either? They are all important, but we are all different too.

With eating, like many of us, what I put in my mouth depends on my emotional well-being. I used to eat granola bars thinking my brain would process faster or they'd somehow make me smarter. I needed to do some mom-script rewriting. My mom is a processed-food junkie so when I got my first apartment I filled my cupboards with what I saw in my mom's cupboards. It was down to brand names too. If my mom bought Ragú® then so did I. You know how I interviewed a nutritionist to see if I should become one when I was reevaluating my dream? Well, once I went out on my own and started investigating my food choices, I had to reimagine what I would cook for myself. I've begun to ask myself: what will nourish me? Some of this has meant reimagining Latino culture food, which has meant changing the way I express my heritage.

Exercise was definitely one of the ways to help reserve or increase my energy as I worked towards my dreams over the last decade, including when I had my identical twins. Walking was my salvation and it still is. There's evidence that walking calms your nervous system. What about you? Can you walk more and use that time to charge your battery? Perhaps there is another form of exercise you can work into your day. If you have time to eat then you have time to move. One working mom I coached wanted to lose ten pounds in thirty days. She lived in a state where driving was the norm and winters bring ice storms. I saw limitless ways she could introduce exercise into her weeks. Yes, she explored some new ideas—however she resisted others. It's worthwhile to muster the energy to make new choices especially in less-than-ideal situations. This has been how I've been able to bring my most fertile ideas to life.

I am the kind of mom who didn't choose to sleep when her baby slept. Are you like me? Being productive gives me energy. Am I weird? Checklists and to-dos give me a high! But you need to find what works for you. Maybe use a smartwatch to monitor your sleep, you may need less than you think. There's lots of information out there about ways to improve sleep if it's an issue for you.

Guilt weighs a lot and really affects our emotional health. Some clients have stayed plugged into American Dream jobs because of the guilt and shame they would feel for quitting. There are lots of moms with emotional burdens that are draining their energy. Whatever regrets you may have as a mom or a working mom, you have to let them go. Regrets are energy vampires. You may regret that you have to serve takeout every week. You may regret that you didn't nurse your son. You may regret having chosen your first babysitter. You may regret that you wasted a decade working in a toxic environment. Let it go.

How can you use your imagination to safeguard eating, moving, sleeping, and emotional health; the things that can help you find more energy in your busy life?

Moms did some incredible things during this pandemic when schools closed. We can make the time for something when it's essential. Your energy is essential because that is the only way you can ever truly unleash your fullest potential. So use your imagination to think about how you can change the way you exercise, sleep, eat, and look after your emotional well-being.

It's important to have an honest look at yourself and give yourself a shot at your dreams by really aiming to care for your own vessel. There is hope on the other side of this equation. You can be pulled, as if by the grace of God, to the right dream for you. So where you may feel as if you have no more to give, if your dream excites you (no BS) then you can find a tugboat to pull you to the finish line. This, more than addressing self-neglect, as DJ Esther taught us, is a smart way to approach our lives. James is showing us the path to optimize ourselves for the battle to achieve our individual dreams. When I interviewed my next podcast guest, Beth Comstock, I told her that I didn't think I had the stomach to ascend a corporate ladder, especially at a place like General Electric. I assumed that working for an industrial manufacturing conglomerate known for leaders wouldn't be a place for someone as weird as I am. It turns out that this idea of being weird was game-changing for both Beth and GE. Seeing how many of my mom peers work in corporate roles for established companies, I want to be sure that you see how stretching your imagination can be your competitive advantage. It's time to play with your reawakened imagination!

Your turn to take what you've learned in this chapter to reawaken your imagination. Use the following section to tailor the lessons you've uncovered from this chapter to fuel your imagination this week.

BIG IDEAS

- Check for the energy drains in your days and limit them as best you can

- Raise your energy levels consciously by focusing on eating, moving, sleeping, and emotional health; take daily baby steps starting today

- Big dreams can energize you but you need to bring your best energy baseline

- Emotions zap energy including regret, worry, and guilt; don't waste your energy on them

IMAGINATION WARM-UPS

1. What support do you need to ensure your emotional well-being is cared for? A therapist, astrologer, church counselor—pick someone to help you uncover the emotional burdens you're carrying.

2. Can you use your imagination to cook yourself and your family the most beautiful and nutrient-dense colorful meals ever?

3. What are some imaginative ways you can think up to find a spot on your calendar every single day for thirty minutes to bring your heart rate up or at least walk?

4. How can you use your former commuting time to catch a catnap? Imagine you had to nap or your battery would die.

5. Your plate is full. What can you imagine taking off that perhaps no one will really notice but you? Hint: worrying takes energy and so does caring about what others think.

II.

PLAY WITH YOUR IMAGINATION

OKAY, SO YOU SHOULD have woken up your imagination, faced your fears, thought about the dynamics influencing your life, and reviewed your mom script, and now you're ready for an update. It's time to play. You are planting seeds and looking for signs of growth when you are playing. As someone without a green thumb, for our purposes, you'll be looking for the activities that make you feel positive emotions. You are also putting your imagination into practice. Trying on mom jeans and seeing if I can make them look cool would be one example of me playing. A fertile imagination is the ultimate superpower. You'll need to learn how to best harness it in your life. The point of reawakening your imagination is to uncover what interests would make you light up like a Christmas tree! (This may mean resurrecting old or uncovering new interests.) In this section we will show you how.

When was the last time you gave yourself permission to explore weird rituals, experiences, or wacky trends outside of your comfort zone? I vote for totally immersing yourself with a playful, open-minded wonder to exploit the value the art of playing can bring into your life. Introducing novel experiences into my life is what has made it extra-exciting. I want to give you permission to do the same. I want you to use your imagination to find your passions, adapt what you already know and do, tap into your childlike self, embrace your impostor syndrome, and have fun.

Since we are playing next, it's also important that we bring in our families. Who better to share our imagination with? You'll hear about how sometimes our imagination can use some extra coaching from an expert or even our own kids. Tag! You're it. I'm ready to play. Let's do it.

Before you start playing, have you downloaded the Imagination Warm-Ups from my website yet? You can even print them! The act of physically writing down thoughts has therapeutic effects. Go wild! Conjure your inner Lisa Frank and use some fun stickers too. Did you also take the free online quiz to uncover your Imagination Wellness Assessment? Find out what's *really* stopping you from getting unstuck and making progress on your best entrepreneurial ideas. It's a fun way to learn about yourself. You'll also find the original podcast interviews featured in this section, playful resources to inspire your imagination (including my original Mo Willems piece, whose backstory you'll learn about later) and my latest updates at:

www.fertileideas.com

Most importantly, you'll also want to join the **Imagination to Impact Five-Day Challenge** (valued at $49, yours for free) to reawaken, play with, and stretch your imagination to discover your most fertile idea. This is where to start to experience firsthand what using your fertile imagination can look like in your daily life with your kids.

Chapter 9

GIVE YOURSELF PERMISSION TO BE WEIRD

-BETH COMSTOCK, A FORMER CMO AND VICE-CHAIR OF GENERAL ELECTRIC

In this chapter you will:

- Think expansively about what you could explore, experience, or enjoy *even* as a mom
- See how someone pushing the envelope can be game-changing and necessary
- Identify new behaviors, communities, and identities that might wake up parts of you that you never imagined having
- Be asked to consider things that might feel weird and pointless
- Explore ideas you can use right now to stop feeling stagnant

ONE YEAR I DECIDED to attend Ad Week in New York City. I had left advertising years earlier so you'd think I would have felt like a fish out of water. I felt as if I had never left. During a break I saw Mindy Grossman, the then CEO of WeightWatchers, interviewing Beth Comstock, a former CMO of GE and the first female vice-chair of GE. I was watching a C-suite level conversation about women in the workplace between two women who rose to the top of their career ladders.

Beth had now left and she had just published her book *Imagine It Forward*. After seeing this interview I felt compelled to ask her to be on my podcast. Based on my experience of getting GaryVee to agree to be a guest, I assumed getting Beth to agree would be as hard as or harder than getting Gary.

So when Beth rapidly responded with a "yes" to my LinkedIn invite I got scared. I felt as if I hadn't earned her time. I tried reading her book and getting interview-ready but I was battling internal resistance. Hello, impostor syndrome! I ended up chickening out and didn't follow up for the interview. The longer I left it, the harder it became to follow up.

It was one year later when I finally gave myself permission to go back to Beth and finally ask again for that interview. This time I was in Australia and by then I had landed lots of big-name guests, so I felt more confident. So when her "yes" came, my "great, let's do it!" was easy to say. My resistance had disappeared.

Why?

I re-engaged with Beth because I was proving a point to a client. My client was hesitant to network with strangers for a job, so I wanted to set an example for her. I figured if I could do this then I'd be helping that client out. Turns out, I got a lot out of that teaching moment. I earned my self-respect back and had an incredible female leader on my podcast.

From Beth I learned that ultimately, the key to playing with your imagination is, first give yourself the permission and second, find someone to hold you accountable. When you use your imagination, the possibilities that open to you can create risks. The risks can be scary.

In Beth's words:

> I came to realize, for me in my career and the colleagues I had, there are always the excuses. Oh, I could never do that. My boss won't let me. Investors won't let me. We don't have the budget. Some of those may have been real, but often when you peeled back the layers what you found was someone was afraid. We don't talk about that in the context of work—being afraid. I came to re-

alize if I'd write an old-fashioned permission slip like in high school, to get out of whatever [class], I could address that fear. So I started carrying some around in a class I taught at GE and I kept a stack of permission slips on my desk. You know, "I'm Melissa...I give myself permission to X."

In Beth's case, she gave herself permission to raise her hand during company meetings. She gave herself permission to ask for help. The latter, according to Beth, was hard for her to do. Deciding to take a different approach to things is a choice and because you may not be in a habit of using your imagination to do so, a permission slip will help remind you. To think beyond the mom or life script that you have inherited you need to use your imagination all the time. Thinking expansively about adventures or interests once came naturally when you were a little girl. So, if you feel as if you've been in a rut then using your imagination will help you feel like you have the power to get yourself out.

To help us discover new paths or options Beth suggests we explore things that are weird, or just outside our normal. But to do so requires you as a mom to prioritize the use of your imagination. This may feel out of character and because it's not habitual yet you may need to add it to your calendar just like you may add a Brazilian Jui-Jitsu class for your kids.

On a holiday to Japan we went to an ultra-fancy restaurant where the menu was unlike anything my husband or I had ever seen. We wanted to taste actual Japanese cuisine, not the Benihana kind we left behind in the U.S. But my boys will only eat run-of-the-mill Caribbean food like rice and beans so getting them to eat anything unusual was going to be a struggle. So we created a Braver Boy Award system for the son who would try anything, even wasabi. Turns out my twins are driven by such arbitrary awards whereas my eldest stuck to the white rice. In this fancy restaurant, as the waitress took our order, we launched the Braver Boy competition. My youngest, who has now won this Braver Boy award quite often, turned out to enjoy sushi. If we hadn't used our imaginations to find a fun way to encourage our kids to try new things they wouldn't have realized that they adore sushi.

What if you are missing out on some kind of ambrosia yourself? Funny, a fellow mom told me this very thing about vegemite, the very weird black Australian spread the locals rave about. I haven't tasted vegemite. It's too weird for me because I can't imagine how anything related to beer and yeast could ever taste good. However, if I acted on Beth's life philosophy I'd probably bite the bullet just to see what the fuss is all about. Onto you: What if you could explore new foods, forms of art, or do adventurous things? What if you could play with your imagination or your taste buds, for that matter? This is a fun example of how giving yourself permission to do weird things can lead you to new and exciting places.

This idea of playing in a "weird" space is one of those imaginative things you will want to give yourself permission to do. I call it weird because I mean something that is different or strange, something you can't imagine you would enjoy or be interested in. Playing in a weird space makes sense. It helps you explore the rapid changes in technology or trends outside of your knowledge base. It can broaden your experience in so many ways.

Beth says this about giving yourself permission to explore weird things:

> I'm just a big believer in getting out and discovering. It's hard to physically get out in the world right now in this pandemic. But we've got the Internet and this idea to get out and discover and to go where things are weird. So that might be one of the things you give yourself permission on. I'm going to read an article that seemingly is so weird, I wouldn't know what to do with it. I don't know. Let's say I'm a marketer. I'm going to read about cryptocurrency or I'm going to read about how to give a tattoo, I'm going to learn something differ-

ent and do it. Just ask yourself, what can I learn here? The reason to do this is because you're just constantly testing yourself to learn new things, to be curious, and to get a bit of a handle on where change is coming from.

Look at all of the oddest things that have taken off. When I interviewed Beth she asked me to walk through this exercise. I presented her with TikTok as a weird example for us to think about during our interview. Who would have thought that short-form videos that appear nonsensical could work for businesses? Imagine being the advertising agency pitching a TikTok campaign for the first time to a risk-averse brand manager? I worked with brand managers at P&G and it's hard for me to imagine them instantly saying yes to an unproven social media channel. The same went for GE, but Beth gave herself permission to see if it was possible to use it in some form.

She asked herself:

What if this takes off? What are ways this might take off? What about this idea of little snippets of videos of people communicating might impact how I do business? Could I interact with customers differently? Could I translate this into how I'm working in my bank? So that's some of what I'm talking about. You go to where things are seemingly a little weird and odd and study them. Partly, it's just to challenge yourself to say, what might I learn from this?

In her book *Imagine It Forward*, Beth mentions how she found herself in all sorts of "weird" spaces, such as a K-pop concert in South Korea. The magic that can come out of these seemingly off-the-wall experiences is for your imagination to work through.

Often I like to take the advice of a podcast guest, especially if it gives me the permission to explore something I've been curious about. It's like I have needed permission to, in some cases, go to weird places. Every so often I like to step into things that are uncommon for me, and one week I followed Beth's advice and really dove in because I wanted to understand what would make me come alive. Some people enjoy making beautiful meals to express themselves creatively, and other people have followed their curiosities since they were a little girl. I took a class at my local library focused on creating fantasy land maps. Think: *Narnia* and *Game of Thrones* (neither of which I'd ever been interested in). So why did I take this class? Why the heck not? I write a lot but I don't draw much at all. I decided to see the world in a new way and see if drawing would stir up something new in me. Here's what I learned about myself:

My imagination is super active. I mean, I was including stockbrokers and investors hanging out at beaches in my maps. I also felt philosophical. My thought was: *oh my God, have I been living in someone else's rendering of a map?* Lastly, my big takeaway was that we can configure the world based on our imagination. Did you catch that last sentiment? Decide to configure your world. Grab a pen and start drawing the world you wish to experience or stay stuck in someone else's rendering. Are you with me?

Australia has a vibrant sailing community. I didn't realize it was known across the world as quite the epicenter of this sport. My decision to take a weekend course to learn how to sail and earn a certificate was another weird thing for me. All of my weird adventures haven't given me my next big business idea but they have changed my perspective. I realized I don't actually like sailing and life on the sea is an entirely different way of being. But it exposed me to a subculture I hadn't met before. I am now aware of these subcultures and I find them fascinating. As a podcaster these random experiences have helped me build a rapport with many guests.

How can putting yourself into a new situation teach you something new about yourself, your society, or life in general? In my case, during the mapmaking class I was calm. Do you know how long it had been, during the pandemic era, since I'd felt pure and utter calm? Sitting in that class touched a part of my brain that hadn't been touched and it's from that place I could reimagine my own business, my podcast guests, or new home decor. Meanwhile, because my time in that fantasy mapmaking class felt therapeutic, I soon read up about how moving our hands has therapeutic benefits. As a result I have asked my clients to skip their keyboard pounding and write out their homework. It's calming.

In the case of my sailing lessons, I saw adults with disabilities smiling on sailboats. This made me think about my nephews and nieces who have disabilities. Imagine if they could spend a day at sea? Imagine how fun and out of the norm that would be for them? I didn't come up with an idea for a new vessel from that weird weekend experience but it's in the back of my head. I'm ready for a conversation about sailing or I can now help a client reimagine their idea delivered on the sea if suitable.

Giving yourself permission to explore the weird can engage your imagination to help you overcome obstacles, cross-pollinate ideas, and expand your perspective as a mom and contributor, from the PTA to the boardroom. The idea that we think anything is weird is just a clue that it runs outside of our mom scripts or those of the society in which we live. The truth is that exploring things outside of our norm is fertile ground for our imagination. Your imagination gathers images, scents, feelings, sounds, ideas from all over the place. The more you are exposed to, the more permutations there are to live your life. Meanwhile, if you ever intend to climb a corporate ladder or build your own professional ladder then this is the edge you need to innovate. It's riskier to be a business that does the same thing over and over than one that keeps you guessing about its latest innovation. Isn't it obvious how to beat a competitor when you know its moves? Same goes here. See what else is happening around you. Give yourself permission to uncover what new trends are out there. It's worthwhile because stagnation is the consequence of not giving yourself the permission to do weird things. Staying in a rut is what happens. Do you want to stay stuck?

You will benefit from exposing yourself to weird things and it's a worthy endeavor. You will learn about yourself. Think about the effort we pour into uncovering what our kids enjoy or are good at. To think that you have already uncovered everything you'd like or excel in before becoming a mom is limited. Like, what if you did enjoy archery? Seems random, but what if taking on that sport did give you a new lease on life? There are authors who aim toward a bulls-eye before sitting down to write. It's interesting and so are you! You deserve to turn your interest inward in the same way you turn it outward toward your kids. Sure, they have more life to live. However, you are not dead! It's important to continuously explore what else might light you up or change your perspective on life.

Meanwhile, imagine the stories you'll have up your sleeve! Think about how you'd feel taking a trapeze class. What if you learn about Web 3.0 and you kinda like it? You could find your tribe! Give yourself permission to explore the world. It's not selfish. Think about this like poking around to see where you are ticklish. Laugh more! Alternatively, if you're a professional, then this needs to be part of your annual plans to keep up and dominate your sector. Why can't YOU be the one to bring in a billion-dollar idea to your boss next year? Is that not in your script? It might be time to rewrite your own businesswoman script too.

Beth is a Hall of Famer in the world of commerce. In the spirit of playing with your imagination, I want to help you consider how you can approach an old interest or craft from a different angle. How can it actually serve you by making you well-rounded and able to see things with a bird's-eye view? You can apply the lessons featured next if you have any interests, hobbies, or former careers that you want to explore for whatever reason. Use this opportunity to play with your reawakened imagination and contribute or participate in a new way. Remember Martha? You may find you are able to plug back in to an old mission or craft with more skills than those who never left!

Your turn to take what you've learned in this chapter to play with your imagination. Use the following section to tailor the lessons you've uncovered from this chapter to fuel your imagination this week.

BIG IDEAS

- Practice using your imagination to make it a habit

- Explore "weird" things like your joy depends on it; sometimes it will

- Give yourself permission to act unlike yourself in the best way

- Working moms, stay-at-home moms, and those of us in between all deserve to shake things up on our terms

- Exploring interests doesn't stop for moms

IMAGINATION WARM-UPS

1. Can you imagine for a moment a book you are curious to read but would be embarrassed to be holding in public? Read that book.

2. Where does your imagination go when you think about doing weird things? Any activities pop up?

3. What sort of trends are you noticing amongst tweens or young kids? Explore one. Then, as you are exploring, ask yourself: what can I learn here?

4. Imagine some ways that you can be held accountable for exploring weird things. Has any type of accountability worked before?

5. Can you list five virtual or digital tools or products that you can explore (e.g., NFTs, bitcoin, anything fueled by Artificial Intelligence, etc.)? As you glance at your list, just imagine thinking: what if this really takes off? Then what?

Chapter 10

EXPLORE YOUR CRAFT FROM DIFFERENT ANGLES

-PHAIDRA KNIGHT, A RUGBY HALL OF FAMER

In this chapter you will:

- Learn about being flexible enough to play out the identity that is closest to your heart

- Play with refreshing ideas, to stay relevant or return to an interest you once loved

- Think about how you can stay connected to your first interest or career choice when you've got different priorities as a mom

- See that there are benefits in experiencing an interest, or playing a role, in different ways

- See how a world-class athlete continues to participate in the world of sports and reaps rewards from her breadth of experience

WHEN WE START on a journey of discovery we're never sure where it's going to take us. Sometimes we need to start from where we are now but then pivot in a different direction.

I began my corporate career at Chase Manhattan Bank, shredding old paper-based performance evaluations in a generalist HR office on Water Street in Manhattan. At the time, I had two opportunities in front of me. I could either switch business units each year or I could deepen my experience in one business area for four years. As a curious person who didn't really see herself in business I decided to see everything I could. Why not? I was eighteen and switching interests wasn't career suicide, it was just being an explorer. It turned out this early instinct helped me in the future. It is why I've been able to quickly adjust my lens as a coach for my clients. As I went from one business unit to the next I realized that although each area had differences in terminology and markers for success there were more similarities than differences. The same human dynamics were at play in both an HR or investment management team and I saw those dynamics both on the inside and outside thanks to the fourteen unique business functions I worked in while at Chase and later in other companies too. All business units are set up to maintain the integrity of their budgets and bring shareholder value. Ideally you want to make more money than you spend. Once I understood the basics I could easily understand my teams' needs. Meanwhile,

I was developing both a bird's-eye view and cross-company view on what everyone else was doing. I discovered there was value in the holistic view that I wouldn't have developed if I'd done a deep dive in one area.

Ultimately if you can do different things you are more valuable. This is also about longevity in a field. If you uncover different ways of participating then you can stay involved for the rest of your life if you wish.

I could not have anticipated how being a curious employee could have helped me, decades later, as a career coach; however the lessons have served me well through the years. My experiences taught me to quickly identify where I could add value by asking key questions. Then, as a career coach with my own private practice, it made it easy to explain to clients how other people would interpret their voices, behaviors, or experiences in a business. If a client had specialized in one role and couldn't see opportunities beyond what they were familiar with, then I could. I would explain to them how their expertise could translate into several roles and add value to their entire dream organization. It's helped many clients position themselves for jobs well beyond their current level. Yes, it even helped one mom apply for a job and also end up with an unanticipated promotion because of this bird's-eye approach. In your life, you may have a particular interest you could explore further, you don't need to try something new to play with your imagination. By expanding current opportunities you may find new possibilities that fit into your life. You could take this further and prioritize what you already enjoy; you may find even more new possibilities. In my coaching practice, I've always enjoyed the challenge of envisioning what else is available.

This brings me to Phaidra Knight. Phaidra is not a mother but I like to learn from anyone who has leveraged their time and skills. This is not suggesting that you ignore your reality, if you do have kids! Instead, this is about thinking more expansively. Show your kids an alternative script or how they can find one for themselves. Phaidra is an athlete who has had an immersive and varied career in sports. In 2017 she was the first African American woman inducted into the Rugby Hall of Fame. She has made three appearances in the Rugby World Cup and was selected as a top player in the world for her position in 2002 and 2006. In 2010, she was named the U.S. rugby player of the decade. In 2010, she also became an avid CrossFit competitor, and in 2013, a member of the United States developmental bobsled team. She's not slowing down either, she competed in her first muay thai competition in 2021, winning a championship belt. In addition to her personal sporting achievements, in 2019, Phaidra founded Peak Unleashed. This not-for-profit organization is dedicated to the personal, educational, and physical development of marginalized youth, especially those incarcerated and exploited, through activities including rugby and yoga.

Phaidra is also a motivational speaker and sports broadcaster and serves on several boards. She has a passion for fashion and is a powerful voice in the quest for equality for girls and women in sports. Phaidra launched the PSK Collective, an apparel line, in the fall of 2020. We spoke right during the time that the pandemic swept us away in 2020. It had just been announced that the 2021 Olympics would be postponed and Phaidra was training for a mixed martial arts (MMA) competition in a remote area in the U.S. Phaidra didn't stop when the world stopped; she adjusted her approach, not her end goal.

Being an athlete is the core of Phaidra's identity. She is constantly training and learning how to optimize her power both on and off the field. The gyms could close and sporting arenas too, yet Phaidra stayed true to her. The pandemic didn't stop her from honing in on her MMA skills and clearly being in her late forties wasn't an excuse either. She's becoming a pro and had five wins and zero losses in MMA the last time I checked in on her.

In Phaidra's words,

> I've always been a strong believer that age is just a
> number. If there's something that you want to do

(maybe you were a college or high school athlete, and you deferred that dream) then there's nothing that's keeping you from going out, training, and going for the goal. I know that there are only a small percentage of people who will actually do that but you can still enter your own world Hall of Fame. There doesn't have to be a formality to it like mine was. It's about pursuing your dream and satisfying that desire inside. I'd argue that desire doesn't really go away. As you get older, it might evolve. But it doesn't necessarily extinguish.

Think about yourself. Could you imagine having a goal to do something physical in your forties or when you turn fifty? Can you see yourself running a marathon or learning how to backflip? What about participating in a team sport? What if something big happens that year? Gyms close. Wildfires happen. Would you find another way to train? Phaidra is truly inspiring. Let's imagine a goal that's more along the lines of being imaginative about your craft. This scenario is one where you can play with your imagination. Let's engage it.

I don't know many boxing moms but I do know many moms who left advertising but wanted to continue to feel creative and bring in revenue for their family. Advertising can be thought of as a profession for young people who have no kids. Many moms left agency life because it was inflexible. Being expected to pull all-nighters in search of the perfect company pitch was common. Travel for client meetings was a normal part of the job.

So what does that mean for women with children (or one child) who don't want to work like that anymore? What if you want to hit Eject on your corporate career? Maybe you already have, but you miss creating smart solutions for business challenges? Your skills and talents can continue to be used and bring value to the only people who often really matter: you and your family. Do you need to go to talent purgatory and never return because your experience is stale? Absolutely not! This is what your imagination was built for. Find a way to hone relevant skills. One mom who left advertising is now a photographer. For those of you who want to leave work completely, you can use your skills with your children. Do not knock the thrill you can get out of immersing yourself into the world of arts and crafts with your kids. Those toddler years as a mom to my firstborn, I had no idea what I was supposed to do with my son, so every day we made a craft. The skills you honed in your pre-mom life, even the ones used in an office setting, can be used at home. This is another way of stretching your capabilities and seeing where you can take your skills and interests. If your identity is that of a creative person then let's now think about this identity in a different way. You had a life before creating a life, we all did, so perhaps you need to look around for others who are doing something a little differently.

Here is how Phaidra thinks about this:

> I think you can learn a lot visually when you can see the pros and cons of other players. You can see a lot of yourself in them. You can also correct those things on the fly. It's something that you have to do when you're doing a game analysis [as I did as an NBC commentator]. On live television, you're talking through what's happening or what should have happened. You certainly learn. It's almost like looking at things through a coach's eyes. I certainly think that any player that's ever coached, while playing, can tell you that they've become a better player. You have to tune into the technical elements of the game. It's almost like training a different aspect of your nervous system.

Imagine how Phaidra would stretch herself if she was a mom who had been the lead singer of her high school band or even a creative professional? What ideas might she play with, using her imagination? Your identity doesn't have to stem from being in the workforce; it could be the identity that you once enjoyed before you had kids. She thinks about goals as a timeless possibility. You can be a forty-five-plus mom and still do as she would, in your own zone of genius.

You can use your imagination to choose what to bring with you as a mom and what to leave behind. Some women leave a bit more behind than is healthy for their sense of self, when they become a mom. They may drop a job or completely stop what once made them feel important deep inside. You don't need to give yourself totally to your kids and lose your sense of self. Your craft or career may have been integral to how important you see yourself. If yes, then again it's important to find a way to stay plugged in. Phaidra stayed plugged into being an athlete and continued sports and eventually her different vantage points helped her holistically; I suggest you do the same.

There is always a way for you to participate in anything that you love. There is also always a way for you to astound yourself in the process and therefore greatly deepen your expertise. Both of these possibilities in my life have created an ultimate level of fulfillment.

This is Phaidra's account of how she enriched her athletic abilities by stretching in all sorts of ways. She's played lots of sports and in those sports played different roles. She has experienced a lot of things she was able to carry over.

I've learned that a lot of positions in different sports transfer over across all sports. Things like athletic positioning is similar across the board for most sports. So when I'm doing mixed martial arts, there's a lot of carryover. There are a lot of different things, but there's a lot of carryover in terms of foot positioning, in terms of hand positioning, in terms of where you look, the alignment of your spine. There are some stark contrasts, but there are also some similarities. So playing rugby and watching rugby has made things far more in tune and adaptable as has my time as a mixed martial artist.

You are training a different part of your nervous system when you do something differently. You will be challenging yourself if you decide to switch the angle from which you are viewing your craft.

Phaidra is awakening others' imaginations. She achieved the big goal of being inducted into World Rugby's Hall of Fame. Phaidra's imagination in action got her to that post. Phaidra said during our interview that because she achieved her Hall of Fame status, other girls can see themselves in her. Phaidra says, yes, it's now seen as being possible for them too if they work really hard to stretch their skills and explore their power in different ways. It's easier to believe we can do something when we see someone like us do it. It's like seeing a mom do a marathon and then challenging yourself to do one. If being a mom isn't a hindrance for one mom then it gives us hope we can do the same. Hope reawakens our imagination too. Hope can be a powerful driver for us. We can be watching thousands of men running but once a mom friend does it, it makes us feel like perhaps we can too.

I had to ask Phaidra how it felt when she was told she was a Hall of Famer after a decade in her sport, and this is what she had to say:

> Honestly being the first African American to be inducted created a pathway for other girls who look like me, are similar to me, are of color, and for other girls who are not straight. Country girls that grew up on small farms and in very small towns in the South or in rural areas of the country. It gave me that validation. I'm proud to take on that title. It now gives anyone who sees something about themselves in me the vision of what they can do, be, and accomplish. They want to play rugby? They can also. When they play, they can probably be inducted in the Rugby Hall of Fame if they work hard enough.

There is always something to work on in the category of your interest, and exploring your craft from different angles will give your imagination a ton of opportunities to play.

Phaidra is an athlete. At nearly fifty years old, this identity could have been ripped away from her and you know what, the world wouldn't think much of it. **Sometimes you may need to set a higher standard for yourself than others would.** Phaidra reached the pinnacle of rugby and she is committed to remaining an athlete and seeing how else she can express her athleticism. What if you could see life on this planet as a school? If you see life that way then it begs the question, what else is there to learn about yourself? How else can you use a pre-mom skill or a skill you explored in your youth in the situations you find yourself in today? You may not want to be a master in your skill, but what if you could astound yourself by seeking excellence in your skill? What if your skill were timeless? Phaidra found an anchor in her life as an athlete. What if you are different? Are you drawn to lots of totally different topics or do you want to pepper your life with wildly different but highly passionate interests? Ever been to Italy? Let's go to Tuscany. I want to introduce you to a Ducati-loving chef who has lived many lives from being a TV show producer, a cookbook author, a chef, a dad, and a farmer. Changing lanes may be a luxury but that doesn't mean we can't live vicariously for a chapter, right? Who knows what insights you can apply in how you approach following what fascinates you.

Your turn to take what you've learned in this chapter to play with your imagination. Use the following section to tailor the lessons you've uncovered from this chapter to fuel your imagination this week.

BIG IDEAS

- Your age shouldn't stop you from claiming an identity or participating in an activity you've enjoyed or want to enjoy
- Approaching an old or former identity in a fresh way makes you well-rounded
- Create your own world-class championship to add an inspiring goal with purpose to your life
- Serve other moms as an example of what's possible for them

IMAGINATION WARM-UPS

1. What is a craft that feels integral to who you are? What sort of things as you are doing them help you feel most like yourself?

2. What aspects of your craft would you like to explore? For example, you may love yoga and be curious about exploring yoga for kids.

3. What if you could take some inspiration from how your craft is done for one audience versus another? Let your imagination run wild, what might that look like?

4. What opportunities might there be to do your craft online versus in person or vice versa or using virtual reality?

5. What things can you imagine pursuing by way of an ambitious goal in your craft (e.g., do you want to do a headstand in thirty days)?

Chapter 11

CHANGE LANES

-GABRIELE CORCOS, A JAMES BEARD AWARD RECIPIENT

In this chapter you will:

- Learn how to use your imagination to change lanes
- Explore ways to de-risk your adventures
- Let go of the thinking that when you're a mom all risks are off the table
- Go through how to know what risks to explore and when to let them go
- See what it might take for you to be okay with not knowing everything yet about a topic that you find fascinating.

HOW MUCH TIME do you take to pick an entrée from a fancy restaurant? Seriously. Does it take you much time? Some women I know read the menu before going to a restaurant. Are you one of those? Well, it just took me one breath to say YES when my husband asked if I'd be down for relocating to Sydney, Australia, from Fancy Town, Connecticut. At the time, we had only purchased our car and house three years earlier and our childcare setup was seamless. PS: neither of us had been asked to make this leap. It was a knee-jerk idea to which I gave a real-time YES!

Do you feel as if you have too much to lose to take a risk? Would it feel risky to change what you know you are good at or your country of residence? You might spiral into worry mode and imagine the bad that could happen. What if you made a mistake and couldn't go back? You could lose your retirement funds or what if you don't like the change? What if you were heading down a career or life path and then all of a sudden you were being pulled in a new direction because your heart wanted something new? How would you handle the situation? Would you see switching gears as a luxury or an obligation?

To be that courageous would be foolish at a later stage of life. But is it? Not everyone thinks about their career or life the same way. Sometimes changing lanes can take you somewhere you didn't expect to go. If you didn't go, you would have missed out on an enriching experience.

"Taking a risk," in my life, has often been code for being audacious enough to go against what other people expect but doing what I secretly have been wanting to explore anyway. It's often led to better stories and new realizations about me than if I'd made less risky moves. My imagination tends to lead me to being riskier than my extended family. I can tell from my own experience that when I've taken a risk it's greatly benefited me and often my kids. However, just like couples can start to look like one another; I think their imaginations align too. The sky's the limit when you pair an optimist with someone with a fertile imagination. As a result, my husband and I leaped into the unknown.

Neither of us had ever even visited Australia. We had just settled in Connecticut. There was no job that we needed to relocate for. We had the luxury of being able to act courageously. We figured out how to get visas to live in a new country and tenants for the house, sell a car, and get everything done within one year. The hardest bits were done in two weeks after our visa was approved. Finally, there we were, flying to Sydney, with ten pieces of baggage and three little boys. We had two sets of hands. Really, think about how we schlepped our stuff at the airports. It was chaotic and messy. This crazy adventure was sparked by an interest. My husband was interested in a different way of experiencing life and I was game. I said yes instantly when he presented this idea. I've thought longer and harder about where to eat dinner than about whether I'd move to Australia. No logistics had been considered. It was a "heck, yeah!" decision.

I am so glad we acted on that crazy idea. As a result of that move, I am more loving and compassionate toward my sons. All of us were new to everything in Sydney. I had to learn how to drive on the left-hand side of the road. A different part of my brain had to be switched on. We found ourselves in the middle of a wildfire season of historic proportions. Then the pandemic happened and luckily we were spared from the worst. Through it all we have grown closer. We've seen life through a different set of lenses. Making this move made me feel like I did back before I had kids and lived in Paris. I couldn't have imagined I would feel so thrilled about exploring the world as a mom. Yes, we get to be interesting too! Imagine feeling that kind of pre-mom bliss in your own way?

Some would agree that picking what your heart desires is a luxury. Gabriele Corcos would also agree. His life experiences are the kind that deserve their own version of Anthony Bourdain's travel and food show, *Parts Unknown*. He made several really significant changes to his life, moving initially from Italy to Los Angeles, then to New York before finally deciding to return to Tuscany at the beginning of the pandemic. We did get to see a tiny slice of his life on his Cooking Channel show *Extra Virgin*, which he produced and co-starred in, with his wife, the actress Debi Mazar.

My conversation with Gabriele began when I asked him about how being a restaurant owner in New York compares to life in Tuscany. It only took him a second to say, "New York is a nightmare." This should tell you why he is one of my favorite and most colorful conversations, he doesn't talk around an issue but is open and honest. This is how Gabriele reached the decision to shut down his Brooklyn restaurant and return to Tuscany.

> My cooking is an act of love. Really, that's the way I always interpreted what I did, and New York stripped that away completely. When I closed my restaurant, I spent a year [thinking]. I tried to think about what I wanted to do with myself and then I decided that I needed to come home. So that was a very important moment. It's not for everybody, especially now in this moment with the pandemic and everything. I hear that 40 percent of restaurants in New York will never reopen again. If it keeps on going this way, it'll climb to 50 percent or 60 percent.

When I interviewed Gabriele, I noticed one key thing: he uses love as an inner guidance system. He embraced this emotion. It had guided him to change lanes and take a completely different journey. I heard Gabriele's ability to trust his heart in his voice. He had met Debi, his future wife, and knew that his love for Debi was not a summer fling. Gabriele was courageous enough to follow his heart, and he had prior experience that helped him. As we learned in Michelle Florendo's chapter, this is often as valid a source of information with which to make decisions as logic.

Earlier on in his life Gabriele loved biology and later percussion instruments, so he traveled the world learning about those. This was light-years before his NYC restaurant and prior to his returning to Italy. Gabriele shared a story about when, after years of pursuing a music career, he had been offered the opportunity to be a back-up percussionist with Shakira's band. If Gabriele accepted this offer, it would have meant being on the road during the first year of his daughter's life. This decision is so common for the moms I've coached, but hearing a dad struggle with this was eye-opening. This is also an example of changing lanes. You may not have the luxury, but if you've made hard career decisions in relation to your family then you already used this muscle featured in this chapter. What if you just used it again? In Gabriele's case, out of his love for his daughter he turned down this seemingly once-in-a-lifetime opportunity. It was interesting to hear him gush about talking to his baby girl in Italian and feeding her pasta, he sounded more like me! He was beyond a doting father; his nurturing tendencies bubbled up in ways we too have felt. Might the luxury of change when some cherub pulls our heartstrings really be a change in our priorities? Maybe the courage Gabriele was using was to go against his "dad script"?

It seems as if love really inspires Gabriele. The key distinction for Gabriele is that he can afford the luxury to follow his curiosities and be courageous. Several concerns may pop up for you based on this difference. What if you don't have the luxury of following your heart? Some of us have made commitments that are hard to break such as signing up for the military to go on tour across the Middle East or becoming a U.S. diplomat who is stationed in parts of the world where the government needs us. Alternatively, you may have bought a house with a huge mortgage that depends on two incomes or agreed to be the sole caretaker of an aging parent. In instances like these, it would be difficult to change your mind or skirt your responsibilities.

In Gabriele's words:

> I realized as I was growing up that as long as you really fall in love with something, it's not about studying, it's about nurturing your soul. It's about growing and enjoying life, and deciding that something is of interest to you, and you just

go for it. So reading a book and loving a book [is an option]. It doesn't have to be studied. But if it (the topic that interests you in that book) sticks with you, if it tickles, if it makes you think, if it helps you change and move forward, or take a step back and look at things with a different perspective, that is of incredible value. You just need to be courageous, which is something that is a luxury.

Do you feel as if you don't have the luxury of being courageous? This is where your imagination comes in handy as a mom. While you may not be able to be a runaway mom, it's not impossible to change lanes if you are intentional about your plans and ask for help. As a mom, you are already responsible for children who keep you on your toes, especially while the kids are small, so it seems like a tall order to explore a new career or obsession. Don't give up hope, though; Martha Hennessey shows us in her chapter that you don't have to do everything now. Maybe later in life you can go nuts and make many changes to follow your interests. Maybe follow Phaidra's advice and work out a way that aligns things with your current schedule or desire to be at home.

So, what can you do instead if you do not have the luxury of quitting your stable job or weekday routine today to join Cirque du Soleil? (Okay, maybe that's too crazy.) Here's an idea: use your imagination to figure out how to "de-risk" your adventure. Don't worry! You get a chance to play with ideas later in the prompts.

As for us, were we crazy when we decided to move to the other side of the world? Yes, but there's nothing wrong with that. Once you follow an interest you feel like a more interesting person. You tend to then do more interesting things. As a result, you attract interesting people into your life. This is expansive thinking at its best. Your imagination is waiting for you to play with it. Yes, this is usually the same case with our kids. Ironically, often they are waiting for us to play. This is usually all they need.

In Gabriele's words, he shares the same guidance with his daughters. This is the way Gabriele has been living his own life.

I've changed my life a few times. This is, I would say, the third time I changed my life or fourth. These scary changes are not for everybody.

It makes me happy because it keeps me on my toes. I like the adventure. I like the fight. Also the emotional aspect of it, the trying to figure out in your head what your next move is going to be, the things that you have to do. And also, the fact that by changing more or less constantly, I am forced to study and learn more as I move forward. So, it is exciting to be back in the country here [in Tuscany]. I'm not a farmer. I'm not a gardener. I don't know much aside from the fact that I grew up here. So again, I took it for granted. I planted this tree when I felt like planting a tree, I do the vegetable garden in summertime, but [I'm] far from saying, let's start designing the right garden for my own next restaurant, that's something that I've never done.

What if the reason you are fascinated by a topic is because you have been put on this planet to be part of its ecosystem? Consider this thought for a moment. Something doesn't have to be practical and instantly obvious for you to feel like you are doing something that may be important. There's a vulnerability in changing lanes and having to learn new skills. There's a learning curve in the change, which Gabriele finds empowering. Many of my clients have been deathly afraid of changing jobs because they think they won't know how everything works. There's this fear of being embarrassed for not knowing everything. To confront and overcome this fear, imagine you are constantly putting yourself in a situation where you may be embarrassed. You are constantly emotionally challenging yourself to come clean with what you don't know. Imagine those situations as empowering learning experiences that make us more resilient.

The parallel to what our kids are experiencing is obvious to me. All of this provides a myriad of opportunities for more candid conversations with them. Change can be scary but bring lots of great things too. You'll also show them how resourceful they can be. How open are you to change? Your imagination will get a kick from being your guide especially if you unleash its power to take you to new territory. So, while Gabriele has explored many lives, in his fifties he is still considering new ones. You may see Gabriele's life as a fantasy, but we can use his story to see that change can present opportunities that make the change worth making. Let love and passion be your guide.

Start with what you really love and head down the rabbit hole to investigate where that may take you. A common risk of changing lanes is a fear of losing what you've accumulated: reputation, wealth, or predictability. **If you were drawn to this book because that little light of yours wasn't the burning furnace it should be, then picking a new lane might not be a luxury—it may be your only option.** Your quest to uncover what nurtures your soul now is as worthy as figuring out whether your child would enjoy playing the trumpet. So many moms don't attach a value to doing something that fascinates them in the same way that they do for their kids. If we want to raise fascinating kids we need to show them what it takes to follow what fascinates us. Sometimes, uncovering what is fascinating to you takes stepping out of the roles you may feel bound by. If you've been a mom well beyond the diaper blowout stage, then you may have forgotten what it feels like to get lost in a moment, forgetting who you were. Your moment may have been up on stage acting in a school play when you felt like a real fairy or while backpacking through Grasse, France, when you felt like a world-class perfumer. Let's step back to when you felt total freedom to see how we can bring forth that feeling into your life and maybe even in time for this weekend. Break out the time machine with me in the next chapter for one of my retro childhood fascinations (and perhaps yours too?). Remember *Sesame Street*? Let's go there.

Your turn to take what you've learned in this chapter to play with your imagination. Use the following section to tailor the lessons you've uncovered from this chapter to fuel your imagination this week.

BIG IDEAS

- The opportunity to learn something totally new is there for moms too
- Use your imagination to de-risk your next lane change
- Don't ignore what fascinates you; if it tickles you then learn more about it
- Changing lanes is not always as scary as you may initially think
- Be a lifelong learner

IMAGINATION WARM-UPS

1. What two or three topics do you find fascinating today? Imagine sinking your teeth into those topics without judgment.

2. Imagine taking a beginner's class on one of those topics. What pops up as you imagine having to learn something totally new? How can you imagine de-risking this option? You may want to find ways to barter in exchange for participating in that class.

3. What if you did have the luxury of changing lanes today? What fears could you imagine stopping you even in that scenario? Any ways you can imagine overcoming your top two fears or reservations?

4. Imagine how your values have changed through the decades. What areas of your life are no longer aligned with your current values or where your heart is today?

5. Where will your imagination take you next? Start with one area of your life that isn't quite fitting in with where your heart is today. What's a no-frills adjustment you can make?

Chapter 12

TRY A NEW ROLE

-CHRIS THOMAS HAYES, A *SESAME STREET* PUPPETEER

In this chapter you will:

- Gain a fresh perspective on your mom role as a character whose biography you get to write

- Feel free-spirited without having to run away to the circus

- Externalize and stretch yourself like an actor playing a role

- Look outside of your mom role, and see what's possible when you adjust new behaviors and even personality traits to your life

- Greatly benefit from allowing yourself to "get in the zone" like children who play with impenetrable focus

ACTING HAS ALWAYS FELT like a skill only suitable for Broadway shows or Hollywood movies, but when I decided to launch my podcast a client suggested I take acting lessons. Apparently, a podcast host needs to know how to improvise, who knew? So I enrolled in a class to learn how. I didn't realize in doing so I would learn how to play again and that sense of play would really help me become the podcast host I wanted to be. Before I tell you about my experience I want to introduce you to Chris Thomas Hayes. I had always had a fascination with *Sesame Street*, especially Jim Henson, the creator of the Muppets. I associate the long-running children's TV show with a sense of play and I was very excited and curious to explore, on my podcast, what it is like to be a puppeteer on *Sesame Street*. Chris performs the jazz-loving, saxophone-playing Hoots the Owl as well as the puppet Elijah, a young Black father. The role of Elijah closely aligns with Chris's own life as he is Black and the dad of a son. Chris took over the role of Hoots in 2019 and needed to both retain the essence of a legacy character and find ways to add his own style, so that Hoots is relevant to the current generation of viewers. Chris embodies the character of his puppet every time and his experience of improvisation and training demonstrates how we can use our imagination to challenge our preassigned script and create a new persona for ourselves.

As Chris says:

> With Hoots, at least early on, it's like getting into the body of something or someone who moves, who's older. Who's a little bit more worn down but not in a bad way. He's seen a thing or two. He's that jazz legend. He's smooth. He's a little bit laid-back. He's not all in his head, like me. And so, it's not just a matter of me going with a script. I'm reviewing the script, seeing what I can pull out that relates to my character.
>
> Improvisation, puppetry, acting, all those things that I learned in my acting courses we have innately in us when we're young. Then slowly, it is dragged out of us, and we become who we are. Then somewhere down the line, we go, oh, man, we used to run around and play and do things for fun.

Although he has a script for guidance, to create the character of Hoots, Chris still needs to tap into a younger, more playful version of himself to ensure the way he performs Hoots is relevant to his viewers. That sense of playfulness and its loss is particularly relevant for moms. **We get so caught up in the stress of day-to-day life that we forget to have fun.** I define playing as when we are totally present in the moment and engage in activities that make us feel free-spirited; like little girls who laugh or pretend to be anyone. We should let ourselves go to that place more often than we do. It would make a lot of heavy mom things feel more bearable. When you are playing, there is no goal. It's about letting our kids or our inner child lead the way. You know the filter or masks we often wear when adulting? Yeah, that filter or mask is in time-out when we are playing. We may not always see the benefits of playing with our kids. I have to think about adding "play with my children" to my list. Meanwhile, my husband plays the role of fellow playmate as if he was made for it. Unlike me, my husband walks in the door and doesn't scour the space for things to pick up and clean; he looks for our chess set to play chess with (and aims to beat) our eldest son. Ever wonder if you could get swept away in play too? It is important not to lose sight of your sense of fun.

Have you ever considered enrolling in an acting class or dabbling in any performance arts as a way of thinking of yourself as a different character? When I took my client's advice about learning how to improvise and feel comfortable talking about myself on a public stage, I enrolled in a course with Adam Wade. Adam has won The Moth's StorySlam twenty times; he is an expert in personal storytelling. The course was immersive and personally challenging. It was out of character for me to do anything like this and it turned out I was the only mom of young kids in the class. The schlep for class from Fancy Town, Connecticut, to Koreatown, NYC, every Sunday afternoon was a pain, but worth it.

It culminated in each of us telling a brief story, onstage, in front of our peers, friends, and families. I wish I could have hid behind a puppet like Chris does. My performance involved a lot of preparation. In the same spirit of getting ready to play a puppet, I told the story of who I was before becoming a mom. To be authentic, I went back to when I was studying and working in France during my MBA. I was living in Paris, in an icebox of an apartment, only eating Comté cheese and grilled chicken and drinking Sancerre wine. I'm sure you can see how foreign that life felt to me by the time I was a suburban mom with three young boys.

As part of an exercise in my acting course we were asked to improvise a story based on a cherished personal object. Mine was an empty fragrance bottle. Toward the end of my three months in France I decided to backpack through the Côte d'Azur. I visited Grasse, the capital of the perfume industry, where I bought myself a bottle of Fragonard perfume. The empty bottle has always reminded me of that wanderlust time in France. I had to figure out how to tap into my pre-mom existence so the crowd could feel how free I felt back then; the bottle was just my way in.

My entire body changed as I told that story. I smiled. I felt as if I was back in Monaco with my heavy backpack hopping on and off trains during my last days in France. In that moment, I wasn't thinking about my long commute home that night or being a mom. When I returned home I was happier and more playful. That class unlocked something in me that I had in France but had been missing in Connecticut.

Imagine those moments in your life when you felt most free. What images are popping up in your mind? Might there be a way for you to act out those moments to feel those feelings again today? You can take an acting class to be more playful or you can go back to the time when you were. We all have those moments that light us up. When was yours? For some of us getting up on a stage and acting could make us anxious. You can infuse more playfulness in other ways, such as creating comical content on social media (I say this because there are moms who consistently make me leak from laughter) or enjoying a night of karaoke with the girls. It can even be doing Halloween like never before and letting yourself get carried away with your own costume. Just remember, is your inner child leading the way or are you?

If you want to dip your toes in the deep end and use the strategies that an actor uses to play with your imagination, then this is the next step to explore. Chris writes a character biography. He wants to know how to approach playing a part, so this goes beyond reviewing the script he is handed.

As Chris describes:

> I have a notebook. I will try to write down as much of a bio as I can think. A lot of it is just me thinking. *He is from New Orleans. He lives in Harlem.* These are just the kind of things that he knows. This is the kind of music he's been around. These are the people he's played with. I'm trying to build a story. I'm building a character without relying on the writers a lot of the time. They obviously could if they wanted to, but I like to have that kind of made-up biography. I think a lot of puppeteers do this. They write themselves a character biography, so they have something to grab on to, especially when you get a script and you're like: how should I approach this?

I know what you're thinking: that exercise makes sense for someone whose job is acting. Hear me out: the next time you wait in the school pick-up line you can use your cell phone to audio record a quick character bio of someone who you would want to swap lives with. In the Imagination

Warm-Ups, I will give you a clear idea of how to proceed. You get to play any role. It's your world, squirrel.

Next, Chris reflects on a suggestion of his mentor that you may want to explore to stretch even further:

> Marty Robinson says to not be afraid to break the glass. He performs Telly Monster and Snuffy and is the original puppet designer for *Little Shop of Horrors*. He's an incredible puppeteer and trains *Sesame Street* puppeteers in other countries. When you have this character, you want to preserve this character that exists, he's behind the glass, and you're looking in. It's important to not be afraid to bring something new. So, I can crack the glass. I can add things that relate to me to this character, and enhance it, hopefully, for another generation.

By taking an acting class or performing like an actor you will be learning how to play again as you once did. Not only should you be having fun, but you can use your playfulness to challenge your script. Create a character that is not like you and play it out. By trying on different characters, you can figure out what works for you. You will also know when you've got it. So how will you know that you are learning how to play like a kid?

You will be in the zone, and it will feel like home. The day of my final performance I was invited to perform first. It was an honor to have been selected to start our show. My family was in the audience. I had over-prepared in the weeks before. My story was about my friendship with a French girl who let me into her Paris; she allowed me to immerse myself in a true Parisian experience. My husband and sons helped me to memorize my lines. When I got onstage, I told my story as if I had just landed back in New York from Paris. I felt at home onstage at the Magnet Theater in NYC. My mom and sister said I looked really comfortable up there. I felt like I was myself; my pre-mom self, for those fifteen minutes. I think I actually felt what Chris describes about athletes who draw on their sense of fun from playing sports in their childhoods.

It's something special when you find someone who can access that [sense of fun] again. Who can have that same kind of fun that they had when they were a kid. I see that when I watch athletes. Athletes on the basketball court or football field. I see them doing what they did when they were little. They are out on the court. They're playing. They're having fun. It's work, but they're in the zone, and it feels like they are at home.

Motherhood is a role. It is like other identities. It comes with its expectations and between-the-lines assumptions. What if you played with the part a bit more? You may not want to take an acting class. However, I invite you to consider what it might take for you to loosen up long enough to enjoy the benefit of dropping the serious mom act. Deep inside you are more than a mom. I'd offer you a few margaritas to get to this depth. However, allowing yourself to feel light and go with the flow a bit more will also do the trick. So what would it take for your inner little playful self to take the reins this week? I sense that you may not be jumping out of your skin to get on a stage. Am I right? If I am, then what follows is a less intimidating approach to playing with your imagination. It's coming to you from the UK and you can use this children's book illustrator's insights secretly. Does that feel more doable— playing with your imagination to change your perception and make nightly book reading a tad more unexpected and interesting, even if it's the 100th read-through? A playful approach for a mom who might be a bit more of an introvert? I've got you!

Your turn to take what you've learned in this chapter to play with your imagination. Use the following section to tailor the lessons you've uncovered from this chapter to fuel your imagination this week.

BIG IDEAS

- Thinking about your pre-mom, free-spirited days can help you today; give it a try
- Playing requires that you let go of control and be fully present
- You are playing the role of a mom; it can be played differently
- There are worthwhile benefits to moms playing; you are missing out

IMAGINATION WARM-UPS

1. Challenge: imagine your own character as a mom. If you could break the glass on your legacy character, then what would shatter?

2. Can you imagine a handful of ways that you can be more playful during a typical twenty-four-hour day?

3. Imagine your favorite childhood cartoon characters and write one biography for your favorite. What parts of their life did you make up?

4. What character would you want to play, if you wanted to imagine another identity for yourself, or to remember a "past life" in which you were perhaps more carefree?

5. Play with the idea of being an actor who gets to play any role she chooses. What role would you play? You could play Princess Leia if you pleased. How would you tailor her bio so that you could feel that powerful and cool? Is there one quality that you'd like to try out just for funsies? Do it!

Chapter 13

USE YOUR OBSERVATION SKILLS

-DAVID ROBERTS, A *NEW YORK TIMES* BEST-SELLING CHILDREN'S BOOK ILLUSTRATOR

In this chapter you will:

- Learn how to be present; take in more of your world

- Recognize it's important to step back and observe a situation from a totally different perspective

- Take off your everyday blinders

- Stop and smell the roses

- Pick up playful ideas you use can yourself and then teach your kids

DURING THE LOCKDOWNS in Australia the libraries were closed. As a result, rereading was our best solution to spending our time in isolation. My sons reread the same Aaron Blabey books over and over again. At the time, I wondered what could my sons possibly be getting out of reading the same stories? Didn't they know the ending of the story? Wasn't the cliffhanger no longer suspenseful? I never imagined that my sons could be seeing these stories with a new set of eyes every single time. My thinking was limited to believing a book could only be imagined in one way, according to the author's words, and those words could only be interpreted in one way. Take for example, one book that we have on our bookshelf, *Sofia Valdez, Future Prez*, which was illustrated by one of my favorite podcast guests, David Roberts. After our chat I realized that when I closely looked at his illustrations, another aspect of the story emerged. On the first read you may think the plot is only about Sofia's quest to protect a park. The second read reveals another story featuring the love and loyalty between Sofia and her furry dog.

What does this have to do with playing with your imagination? The easiest way to engage your imagination is by observing the world. Go back to the children's books you loved as a child with a fresh set of eyes and a clear intention to understand what else they might be trying to tell you today.

David Roberts is the *New York Times* best-selling illustrator behind the *Questioneers* series written by Andrea Beaty. His signature style is rich and detailed, reminding me of what you'd see in a fashion house rather than illustrations in picture books. There's a reason for this. David loves fashion and began his working career as a milliner. He also trusts that a child's sense of imagination is plentiful. David pointed out how he reads the author's story and then goes on to think about how the illustrations can create another dimension to it.

Here is how David puts it:

> As illustrators, we are observing. One of the greatest things that you have is your eyes, to look with. You are observing all the time the things that are going on around you. You are taking it all in, from different people that you might see on the bus or on the tube or as you're walking around. You are seeing different things, pieces of furniture, maybe buildings that you didn't see before. You take it all in.

Try this with your collection of children's books. Open your eyes to see them in a new light. I did this out of necessity. One afternoon I was reading to my sons *Don't Let the Pigeon*

Drive the Bus! by Mo Willems, perhaps for the hundredth time. One evening, during reading #457, I noticed the protagonist in the book, a pigeon that keeps asking to drive a bus, also appears in other books written and illustrated by Mo Willems. This pigeon pops up in ice cream cones at the back of some books or camouflaged in other imaginative ways in Mo's other books. This made the story fresh to me. I began to imagine what that pigeon might be trying to say to me. Was the bird talking to me? Was the pigeon trying to tell me to pursue my dreams? I'm not interested in driving a bus. However, I began seeing it like the dreams we had as kids or once had that we never pursued. Maybe it was my dream to be a copywriter? My imagination did run off with this persistent pigeon. I then began reading the words on the page to my sons but in my imagination it got me thinking that Mo was talking to me about something entirely different.

You can even use your imagination with trash and see opportunities to use it differently. Our kids do it all the time. Have you ever given a young child a paper towel tube? In my case, my sons have created totem poles or telescopes out of them. This is why David's story resonates with me so much. Kids see other possibilities in trash, and for David this is how he realized his passion for creating things. As a kid, David's imagination would come alive on its own simply because he would be surrounded by objects that awoke his creativity.

David fondly recollects his visits to his grandmother's in particular:

> My grandmother would give me a toilet roll. Then I could go into the stock, and then her sewing cupboard, and choose a bit of trimming and stuff. I would then make what in my mind was the most glamorous lady, or a king or a queen, out of this toilet roll, I'd draw a face on it and then dress it with all these little bits of trimmings and stuff like that. That just kept me entertained. I've never forgotten that. I must have been probably five or six, quite a young age. I've never, ever forgotten that way of using these things that look like bits of rubbish to then create something in your imagination that becomes this wonderful, glamorous thing in my mind. I was always creating a glamorous lady or queen, Queen Elizabeth the I, or something like that. It's those sorts of things that can almost feel like little bits of throwaway that can be really important in sparking your imagination.

Imagine this: how this can work in a situation where you want to borrow your child's innate ability to be an expansive thinker? Have your kids ever stopped you to observe things you hadn't noticed?

Even David is surprised when his nephew picks up on new things from David's favorite children's books.

> I'm always amazed by the things that he'll say and the things that he'll pick up on in stories and the questions that he'll ask about stories. I don't just read my own books to him, I read books by my favorite authors and illustrators, and he'll ask something, Oh, why's that? What's that character doing? Then I have to stop and think, oh, I don't know why. Then maybe we can tell ourselves a little story about why that character is doing that.

Try this when it's reading time in your home. Pick any picture book from your child's shelf. Challenge yourself. Use a frequently read one. This time go into your whole routine with a fresh set of eyes. Use your observation skills like an illustrator. Rather than read the story as you would. Why not observe the pictures more closely?

David talks about his intentional layering of stories:

> One of the things that I always do in my work is try to tell a little story alongside a story. Often you might find a little mouse that might continually be throughout the book, in pictures in various places

and things. Or, maybe the mouse is repeating some of the things that the characters are doing in the story? Or maybe not, maybe they're just doing something. You could go back into the book and really look and see what you can discover and see—perhaps what stories you can tell. For instance, one of the books I illustrate, Rosie Revere Engineer, she is a great engineer. She's always coming up with ideas. She's always inventing things. So you could take the character, and then maybe ask your kid, what do you think you'd like to invent? What if you could invent something with Rosie, and then maybe you could tell yourself a story around that?

As you can see, David, and I'm sure other illustrators, depicts all sorts of objects and drawings that can be interpreted in multiple ways, especially because it is common for kids to reread their favorite books.

Your turn: Ask your kids to take on the point of view of a secondary or tertiary character. Alternatively, you can imagine the situation from the point of view of an object. Use your observation skills. Encourage your child to share what they are observing too. This is the kind of active reading that many educators suggest that we apply in our homes. For me, when it comes to Mo Willems's pigeon series of books, I ask my kids tons of questions about the images on the page, the facial expressions of the characters, and even if they would have written alternate endings. Why not use your observation skills together? Let yourself go. Imagine with your child. Now we know that illustrators even draw images to facilitate this behavior.

What might that book be trying to tell you? What hidden messages do you think the illustrator or author is trying to share? If the book is a part of a series then are there any themes between the books? The key is to apply your critical thinking skills and a fresh set of eyes to the children's books that draw you in. Your eyes will know what to look for. Consider this writing exercise like you are trying to crack a code, a code to what will unlock your imagination and elicit a sense of awe and wonder. You'll have a turn in the Imagination Prompts to do this exercise.

A huge benefit of unlocking your imagination is that you will be able to feel that sense of awe and wonder at the drop of a dime. You don't have to be an illustrator for these skills to come in handy either. As a writer, I have found that images have served as some of my best writing prompts. You can learn a great deal about how you see the world and yourself by doing this. I decided to write about that damn pigeon. I wrote and published an article about what I thought it was trying to tell us adults about our lost dreams. The process reminded me about my ambitions to be a copywriter. It's been decades since I had that thought. I got positive feedback from readers who enjoyed my take on a children's book. If the piece hadn't been read by anyone in the world then the outcome would have been worthwhile anyway. I uncovered a skill in me that I value in others. When I've challenged myself to make new observations and think more critically about them, I've been able to quickly pluck out fresh insights that have helped others expand their perspective on what they can do. I find signs of encouragement when I'm that present. That exercise and the public reaction I got encouraged me to express the ideas in this book. What if you had a skill that you admired buried deep inside of you? Do this exercise! There's a reason why the children's books you enjoy or keep going back to are the ones for you. Use this opportunity to uncover why that might be.

David's point about using his observation skills is transferable to your everyday life. This is how, for David, joining forces with someone who brings a different set of eyes has helped him professionally to make a better product. Whilst working with a book editor, David received some constructive feedback about his illustrations of a castle made of chalk by a little boy architect.

David recollects how the feedback helped him make the castle more mind-blowing:

Let's really hammer home this idea. Iggy is a great architect. So I went away and looked at castles and I ended up copying the one based in Austria. It's the one that they based the Disney fairy-tale castle on. The one that is sort of white with blue pointed roofs, turrets, and everything. Then this castle became this huge thing. Now, that sort of feedback is brilliant, because it takes your initial idea, and expands on it, and helps you grow it into something better.

Can you see how using your observation skills like an illustrator could help you in many ways? You have an expert in your home to help you too. Your child can help you see new possibilities. Once you get good at this then you can grow into something better at home or work. Do this work and you will create something mind-blowing too.

To play with your imagination is to nurture it for when you need it. You don't want to lose it because it's not being used. The art of playing in this chapter helps you use your imagination more effortlessly through practice. You will later read about how to stretch it. It's your turn to play with your imagination this time during bedtime. There are many benefits to turning on our imagination especially as moms; we can all agree that being a mom is not a one-size-fits-all type of role. Your imagination is what will help you figure out what you need to be happy. We all want to be happy and uncovering that perfect cocktail of happiness will require the use of this superpower.

David's guidance for me is about engaging with a moment: reading a book to your kids or walking down the street. So many moms want to be more present, and this is your way in. So much can also be learned from Hollywood! The next chapter is about my podcast guest who was a Sundance winner and who has taught me about being single-minded and going after what you want even to the point of defying the experts and putting your own skin in the game. If you don't believe in your dreams then honestly don't expect anyone else to. Let's play like a screenwriter and see if you can apply the kind of thinking that landed Diane a Sundance on her first film. Yes, you can play with your imagination and reap real rewards in the most competitive markets too.

Your turn to take what you've learned in this chapter to play with your imagination. Use the following section to tailor the lessons you've uncovered from this chapter to fuel your imagination this week.

BIG IDEAS

- Your favorite childhood stories might have answers you seek today
- Observation skills can help you practice the art of being present
- Using your imagination is a skill that can be practiced
- Awe is at your fingertips
- You can reread a book or resee a movie and get something totally different from it

IMAGINATION WARM-UPS

1. Imagine your three or four favorite children's authors or books. List them.

2. Observe them with a new set of eyes. What can you imagine the illustrator trying to say in them?

3. Read them and come up with a new set of questions to ask yourself or your child. What made you come up with those new question sets?

4. Imagine writing a comparative piece between your two favorite children's books. Write it. What do they have in common? What's different?

5. What can you imagine that these books are trying to tell/teach you personally at this stage of your life? What actions will you take?

Chapter 14

BE SINGLE-MINDED

-DIANE BELL, A SUNDANCE FILM FESTIVAL WINNER

In this chapter you will:

- Really see how nothing is impossible when you know what you want

- Appreciate the power of being focused and all in on one thing

- Learn how to visualize the affirming qualities you need

- Play with your imagination by jumping into the deep end of the pool and learning to swim even if the lifeguards think you should be in the shallow end

- Understand the importance of being single-minded

WE ALL HAVE GEARS. When you accomplish something big you may feel as if you were operating in a gear that draws power from somewhere, but you aren't sure where from. It's our imagination taking control, when something has to be figured out. You use this gear when you commit to an outcome. You decide to go for it, yes, even if it sounds impossible.

A friend who is a single mom decided on her fortieth birthday to attend a month-long yoga course on a Caribbean Island. The thought of going away for a month as a single mom sounds impossible even to many coupled moms like me. Guilt pops up. The logistics feel too hard. We might check our sanity. Telling those around us might not help either. We fear being judged as a bad mom. "What, you are going on vacation? You are going to send a bad message to your daughter," we imagine people thinking. My friend was determined. She had discovered mindfulness and yoga in her thirties; she wanted to challenge herself and change her life. She really wanted to become a yoga teacher. So she decided, a year in advance, to spend one month in a humid Caribbean tent instead of spending two years driving to local trainings to become certified as a teacher. She shifted into a gear to make her dreams come true. She got into the gear that tapped into her imagination. There were logistics to figure out. Ultimately, she divvied up childcare between her parents in New Hampshire, her aunt in New York, and her ex-husband in Spain.

We all can achieve our dreams when we set our minds to it. This is also where your imagination needs to be your superpower to help you become single-minded in your focus. It turned out that both my friend, who is now certified, and her daughter benefited during this time apart.

This brings me to Diane Bell. Diane is a Sundance Film Festival award-winning screenwriter and director. Her first feature film, *Obselidia*, won two awards, and went on to play at festivals around the world and be nominated for two Independent Spirit Awards. In Diane's case, she decided to write her first script for a movie; she hadn't yet cast herself for the role of a mom. She would not become a mom until her second movie. Diane wasn't a Hollywood insider either, she was a yoga studio owner in Barcelona. She had no formal screenwriting training. She also didn't have the funds to catch flights to meet movie executives to pitch her idea. Diane's story shows us that when we are committed to an idea that "impossible" does indeed become nothing. Who knew?

This was Diane's experience with making an impossible film:

> Making my first film was like a catalog of impossibles achieved. Early on, I had this idea of making the movie. I'd written the script, I had

this idea of making it for $100,000. I thought I could raise $100,000. I wanted to set a budget that showed my film could be made for that amount of money. I gave it to this one line producer, a very experienced person who read it and said to me, Diane, it's not possible. It's literally not possible to make this movie for $100,000. It's at least a million dollars to do it. Well. Wow. I thought okay, fine. That's fine. That's your opinion. I'm going to do it for $100,000. Bye. So, we just parted ways.

Imagine yourself in Diane's shoes. Imagine something you've secretly wished you could do. One way to uncover this hidden wish is to ask yourself: what would I want to do if I wasn't a mom? (Remember, we are playing with your imagination. Save being practical for later, in the prompts.) I've been a mom for eleven years and to truly consider what is available to me I have to stretch my thinking into the unrealistic realm. When you feel confident to let your imagination be your guide, you should trust your ability to tailor this crazy ambition to your life. Imagining something outlandish should not scare you. It's data. You can manipulate data to serve your needs and those of your kids. So rather than limit yourself by thinking that making it happen seems ridiculous, blow the roof off of what's possible. **Sometimes you need to be unreasonable with**

your asks to get what you really, really want. The best part is that once one mom has her unreasonable request met then other moms will too. Worry about your responsibilities and limitations later. Earlier chapters have plenty of resources that can help you tailor your dream to your days. You may have to let go of something in your mom script to add that richness we all desire in our lives.

If I could play Man of La Mancha for a second and dream an impossible dream then I would likely enter a breakdancing competition. It was a thought, and that's about it. However, I don't want it badly enough. I'm unwilling to shift into that gear where my imagination would help me make it happen.

Wanting it enough is a huge distinction that Diane made about the difference between a screenwriter with a film versus one with excuses.

> I think so many screenwriters are not really willing to get sort of uncomfortable. I always have this thought: how far are you willing to go? To make it happen? How much are you willing to invest? If you're not willing to invest that much, why should anybody else? People say to me all the time: I really believe in my script, but I can't get anyone to read it. I can't really afford to go to

film festivals…I can't do that. There are a lot of can'ts. Yet, if you really believe in it, if you know it'd be a good movie and it will sell, then why wouldn't you make it happen?

The way Diane felt about her movie was how I felt about nursing my sons. After their birth, I committed to exclusively nursing the identical twins for one year as I had with their older brother. My decision came with consequences. My pediatrician wasn't happy with their growth rates according to the WHO growth chart. But my sons were giggling and growing. Commentary from the entire peanut gallery tried to convince me to turn to formula. I was fed formula, my husband too, and it felt as if everyone in the universe wanted me to opt for formula-feeding. Looking back, that entire year felt impossible but more to everyone else than to me. I had to use my imagination to achieve my personal goal. My boobs are my business and so are yours; I'm not saying you should do as I did, but this was my experience and it felt as impossible as getting a Sundance Award in my eyes.

A lot happened this first year of my twins' lives. I once found myself pumping milk in the funeral director's private office during my stepmother's funeral. My mom was sent to a mental health facility for months to clean her system of psychotropic drugs and stabilize her mind. In both cases I had to be apart from my twins to meet other family responsibilities. So what did I do? My imagination had to kick in. When it did, I took my embarrassment of tandem nursing my twins off the table. Also, I redefined what success looked like for myself as a mom who wanted to nourish her babies with breast milk. Your imagination kicks in when you leave it no option to abort a mission.

I hired a lactation consultant to ensure that I wasn't crazy. Turns out, I was producing the right amount of milk. So then what? How could I handle being away from my sons? I got creative. A friend from elementary school had twin girls and she was producing so much milk that she had a cooler to spare. Literally a cooler, like the one you take to a beach, filled with frozen breast milk. When I heard her talk about her stash I asked if I could have it and use it for my two boys. I had known her for decades. We had gotten a tattoo together back when we were eighteen and to think she'd be my breast milk angel? I couldn't have predicted this (her name happens to be Angela).

I nursed my sons seemingly nonstop when I was with them, which was 99 percent of that year, then pumped to increase my production when I was not with them. In emergencies such as schlepping to hospitals or attending to funeral matters I would then use that donated breast milk. That year felt impossible. I was often told to give up my personal mission. Clearly, if my sons were not thriving I would have changed my plans. However, I listened closely to my intuition. I was looking at their faces 24/7 and my sons were growing. I'm tiny. If I had married Andre the Giant then I could see how their growth was off, yet my husband was also tiny as a child (he shot up by prom), so they were never going to be enormous. I trusted my instinct and got some relevant advice.

So how can we learn from Diane to help you be that committed to achieving something great that you want for yourself?

Diane says this:

> I get single-minded, singularly focused about a project or something. I believe it is happening, no matter what! It's going to happen, no matter what! It's inevitable. There's nothing that can stop me at that point, nothing. Whatever comes at me, I will find a way around it, I will find a way past. I will find a way through it.

What is a dream you wish to achieve? Have you decided to make it happen no matter what? Or are you leaving things to chance or the outside world? So many of my clients give away their power in this very way. Diane didn't let an expert get in her way from making her film. She wanted to make her movie her way. Once she made this decision she was in control. Once you let anyone else have a say, when they are not directly involved, you are putting your dream in jeopardy. You have to own your dream and your process. This is essential especially for a mom who has a lot of responsibilities and opinions to consider. So what are some practical steps you can take after you've committed to a dream or idea?

Diane, who draws on her experience as a yoga teacher, lays them out:

> I think being in your body, physically, and starting to breathe, and accepting nonjudgmentally your body in itself is a really powerful first step. Then for me, specifically, the affirmation that got me through writing the first draft of my first screenplay ever, was "I am a talented and prolific writer." I started with that information when it was so far-fetched, and my brain was saying, "oh, you're a liar, you're not talented, you're not prolific." And I would go, okay, I hear you brain, that's fine. I'm saying this and I'm going. I'm going to keep saying this. I'm going to keep imagining it. I'm going to keep feeling my way into it. I would imagine how it would feel to be a talented, prolific writer.

If you have never tried any breathing exercises, then simply be mindful of the way you are breathing right now. Is your breathing shallow or deep? Take a yoga class. Do a sitting meditation. As a meditation practitioner-in-training, I've seen a ton of benefits. Or if you are fidgety like me then do a walking meditation. Your body has the ability to take what's in your imagination and bring it out to the world through the use of your senses. You'll need to be okay with your body to do this.

Diane wrote an affirmation about the identity that she wanted to own. Write your own affirmation. As humans, we tend to do what supports the identity that we have. It's time to break from that script. Let's say you want to launch a yoga business. You might use the affirmation "I am a savvy wellness business leader." So what would it feel like to be a savvy wellness business leader? In my own coaching practice, I've stretched my clients' imaginations to take this idea even further by asking really tangible questions such as: What would a savvy wellness business leader be doing on Saturday mornings? What magazines might she be reading? Imagine how such a person might dress.

This is how Diane explained her process:

Whatever your dream is, sit quietly, close your eyes, if you want, and just imagine. Let your imagination go a little wild with what that dream is, what the feeling is. We think we want a certain kind of outcome, but it's always because of the feeling that we'll get because of the outcome. Whatever you want, it's really to do with the feeling. So, what is the feeling? For me, I would have this image: I just had this feeling of freedom, this feeling of being in my flow, being in my zone. You just imagine it. You just enjoy it. Whatever you are called to, it's for a reason. I feel like it is your true destiny.

What might be possible for you if you are single-minded? Do you have a book in you? What about a documentary? Is there something that makes you climb out of your skin because it's so unjust? You can learn from Diane and decide to create or live out your dream even if the world doesn't see it as possible. Take the next steps to see that it happens no matter what. Focus on the right affirmation for you and tie it to your desired or required identity. Then take action when you feel the end-goal feeling Diane mentions. Make your dream a reality. While Diane was pursuing that feeling of freedom she did struggle with impostor syndrome, but she didn't let that stop her. What if you could really play with your imagination and find a way to use it as an asset? What if it could be your business card—the kind that gets people to watch, to join you and help you on your path to success? You'll need to go to Australia to read about how the "entrepreneur's entrepreneur" managed to use impostor syndrome as an asset; Lisa Messenger is up next.

Your turn to take what you've learned in this chapter to play with your imagination. Use the following section to tailor the lessons you've uncovered from this chapter to fuel your imagination this week.

BIG IDEAS

- You have gears and can use them to break through any hurdle
- Affirmations work if you repeat them more often than your limiting beliefs
- Impossible turns out to be nothing for those who are single-minded
- Invest in your dreams first or else they won't happen
- Trust yourself more than an expert about what you are capable of

IMAGINATION WARM-UPS

1. What if you could pull off your crazy and wild dreams? Imagine that!

2. What might it feel like to actually get what you desire and what precisely would you visualize seeing in that moment of accomplishment?

3. Can you imagine five different ways you could approach one of your most impossible dreams?

4. What sort of daily mindful practices can you introduce into your day to support your wildest dream?

5. What affirmations might you need to write and start rehearsing?

Chapter 15

TURN IMPOSTOR SYNDROME INTO AN ASSET

-LISA MESSENGER, THE FOUNDER OF *COLLECTIVE HUB*

In this chapter you will:

- Learn how your impostor syndrome could be your biggest asset

- Not let the feeling you're not qualified, experienced or talented enough stop you. Nothing beats experience.

- Have an opportunity to fast-forward if you've ever felt left behind professionally

- Realize that some ideas have expiration dates; they won't all wait for you to feel ready

- See that people like to help you if you ask

WHEN I TOLD an extended family member that I would become a career coach it felt like an uncomfortable conversation. She asked me what I had done to start pitching my services as a coach. "You didn't get a degree in coaching?" To which I answered: "I've been coaching my peers since 1997 with a lot of success and that's enough for me to call myself whatever I wish." If I were attempting open-heart surgery then clearly the proper credentials are in order, however if you have results in your back pocket related to a field then the easiest way to break into a field is to start calling yourself the title. So many moms take on new responsibilities as volunteers, succeed in them, and yet still feel like they are not actually qualified to charge for them. Results qualify you. If you need to build results, look for opportunities to strut your stuff for free, in exchange for testimonies that highlight your results. Pro tip: you can stop at three testimonials.

Is your lack of confidence holding you back? Maybe you're successful but you think it's just been as a result of good luck, ignoring your skills and hard work. Many moms, especially those who have a business idea but no relevant experience, hesitate to launch or charge due to a lack of confidence or impostor syndrome. This lack of experience is the reason many of us don't use our imagination to create a commercial product or service. Instead, we do nothing or give our skills away for free.

Australian podcast guest Lisa Messenger says being open about her lack of experience when she launched a glossy magazine was the key to her entrepreneurial success. Lisa is the founder, CEO, and editor-in-chief of *Collective Hub*. She launched *Collective Hub* as a print magazine in 2013, with no experience in an industry people said was either dead or dying. *Collective Hub* has since grown into an international multimedia business and lifestyle platform with multiple vertical channels across print, digital, events, and education—all of which serve to ignite human potential. Five years and fifty-two issues into the print magazine Lisa shut it down and pivoted. Since then Lisa has created over sixty books, journals, affirmation cards, online and offline master classes, retreats, and more.

I caught up with Lisa when she was in Austin, Texas, working on the expansion of her brand into North America. In Lisa's signature style, she was writing in real time about her business-building adventures and will publish the book once she lives out its final chapter. This is what makes Lisa different from the other entrepreneurs I've interviewed...Lisa wears her inexperience on her sleeve. She has figured out how to leverage that inexperience, by applying her imagination playfully, and use it to create publicity.

What if rather than fighting feeling like an impostor every single day you could use your imagination to make it work for you too? Our kids play "opposite day" all the time; we can too.

Lisa has been telling the world about her inexperience in media since day one which feels opposite to what many business founders typically do. As Lisa put it:

> When I launched the first issue of that magazine, in my editor's letter, because I'd never been an editor, I wrote something like: "this is my vision." It was really big and lofty, right? Then the second part, and probably the most important part or in equal measure, was when I wrote: "and I have absolutely no idea what I'm doing." The print mag went on to be in thirty-seven countries within eighteen months, the U.S. being one of them. It generated some quite visual success in quite a short period of time, and because I said up front, I have no idea what I'm doing, it got some momentum. I told people, oh, my gosh, this is what happened and this is how we got this cover star or my gosh, this is what happened here. I think I became a bit of the pinup girl for, like, not really knowing anything about too much, but actually having success.

Lisa demonstrated there is a benefit in telling people you have no idea what you're doing. It can generate a buzz around your efforts. This could feel really risky, but you need to have self-belief. I always tell my clients and peers that they are not out there selling snake oil. You are not trying to dupe clients.

One of my peers was an architect who decided to retire from practicing when she started her family. Our calls often took place in hilarious settings and will feel familiar to many moms. Our parked cars become mobile offices and cafeterias, places where we take conference calls undisturbed. This client had a spark of an idea to make a better bag for yoga mats. As usual she was taking our call in her car as she waited in a parking lot for her kids to finish an afterschool program. Sound familiar? My aim on that call was to help her clearly articulate her origin story for her yoga mat bag business. She was hesitant to tie in her architecture experience and focus on form and function; to her it didn't feel relevant enough. Yet, in my mind, I saw that connection as enough to give her the credibility she needed to own her spot in the yoga accessories category.

As a coach for moms, it's clear to me how prior work or personal experience is often enough to launch anything. Sometimes not knowing the business is a good thing, especially if you want to create a disruption or make a PR splash like Lisa. In the case of this yoga mat mom I wanted her to overcome her lack of confidence by leveraging her prior work experience, but after my interview with Lisa I realized that there is also a way to leverage being a newcomer in a market. The key instead may be to simply be brave enough to tell others why you aren't as confident which is often simply due to a lack of experience (not for lack of a solid idea). I've decided to step outside of the box and wear my heart on my sleeve a bit more during the new chapter of my business. Did you know this is my author debut? Imagine: what would be possible if you dipped your toes in a market where you had little to no experience?

Lisa asserts that there are benefits in telling others about your lack of experience. She said:

> A lot of people say to me: oh, my gosh, I feel like you're just like me. That's such a beautiful thing to hear. It is because I don't hide anything and I tell it as it is. I think when we do that, we become relatable and attainable. We give people permission to shine and we give them permission to see possibilities that they may not have previously seen in themselves.

So maybe it's not your plan to launch a worldwide media empire like Lisa. How can you use your imagination to turn around what has stopped you from moving forward? How can you make up for lost time? I ask this because many of us moms feel like we are behind the eight ball, especially if we paused our careers when we had our kids.

This is how Lisa has done this:

> So many people write a hundred-page business plan. They get everything ready. By the time it's finished, the markets have moved on, they've run out of time, they've run out of money, and all sorts of other things. Instead, I test and iterate across social media or other platforms or speak to people all day every day. When I say fail fast, that means I can test very quickly. Is the market interested in something? I get a good gauge of when there seems to be something there. They seem to be willing to pay that price or whatever, then I'll test it. But then I will put a version of it into the market. If it doesn't work, I'll just fail and iterate whatever else and move on. So, fail fast.

The fact Lisa wasn't afraid to tell the world she doesn't know what she's doing made her endearing enough for people to want to help her. It also gave her permission to fail and in front of others. Sir Richard Branson is one of Lisa's biggest fans, and he publicly named his company Virgin as a signpost that he was also a novice. Your imagination can be put to profitable use if you take this concept on board and use it. There are many other examples where I've seen this at play. Imagine that there's a new mom in your kid's school who looks lost on the first day. Wouldn't you want to help her find her way fast? We like helping newbies in so many aspects of life and business isn't any different.

Being open about your lack of experience gives people a chance to feel helpful. If you are open with your feelings of thinking you're an impostor and use it authentically, like Lisa, then doors will open up. Although Lisa has been in business for over twenty-one years, as she expands into the U.S., she is leveraging her inexperience in the U.S. market to learn about how her customer avatar in America is different from her Australian one.

As Lisa put it:

> I think it really comes back to relationships and understanding. Relationships with the right people, who can open the right doors, have already built the networks, and can help to fast-track everything. That's probably something that I've learned with age and stage of business rather than having to do it all myself. I've had to get

very clever and strategic about really appointing the right people on the ground here [in the U.S.] who have the right smarts and the right ways to get in. The best thing that I can do, really at the moment, is to build relationships with them and really understand the nuances of the cultures. I do not want to come here being arrogant, thinking that I know what's best. I want to listen to them and then I want to create products accordingly.

Use your impostor syndrome as an asset. You can use your imagination for anything if you go into business for yourself. The key, however, is to be clear with the help you seek and when you get advice to honor it, if it makes sense for you.

Take Lisa's specific ask:

At the moment, I'm very specific in the U.S. about exactly what we're doing. We're trying to grow the brand. We're trying to grow the footprint. We want as much distribution here as possible. As soon as I say that, and then I tell people exactly what we're trying to do, people jump out of the woodwork to help. People are so generous. Whereas if I keep it to myself, I feel like I'm never going to attract the right people and it's going to be a really lonely journey.

So often moms will ask me for productivity hacks and to their disappointment asking for help is one that I swear by. People want to help you, and if you don't open up about the kind of help you need and initiate the conversations, often with strangers, then you are making it harder on yourself and you will take longer to accomplish your goal. The yoga mat mom happens to be close friends with a mega podcaster who features entrepreneurs on his podcast all the time. My advice to her is the same for you, if you have a business idea: engage your entire network and shamelessly ask for help. My hope is that this mom has the guts to ask that podcaster for a strategic partnership or guest appearance; these requests aren't favors in my book. If you are like me and the yoga-mat mom you'll need a boost to catch up with business owners who never took time off to mother.

When I set out to interview GaryVee and James Altucher on my podcast I decided to tell the world that I was asking them and hoping to have them on my podcast. It was public. You can read about my one hundred days on fertileideas.com today. After day eighty-eight I was losing hope that I was going to get either Gary or James. As a cynical New Yorker, I started to assume it had been a publicity stunt—Gary had offered to be a guest on anyone's podcast if they created a podcast as a result of his interview with James Altucher. I suddenly thought he wasn't going to make good on it. I felt so embarrassed putting it out there but I wasn't dead yet so there was still time. I reminded myself just asking someone to be a guest required balls. I reminded myself that even if I didn't land them, I was doing my best! At one point, I decided to use my client base and ask them for help. I opted to do the unthinkable; I called my former clients and told them what I was up to. Ultimately, I rang a former PR executive for a footwear brand in NYC to tell her about my grand scheme to land GaryVee. I made an ultra-clear request: if she saw GaryVee or could connect me to him, would she call me immediately? It turned out a month later, my client did something she had never done before. She didn't know Gary but when she found herself sitting near him at the Los Angeles airport she approached him and asked him to send me a video message. Gary told me, in his video message, that we would indeed meet at some point, and he thanked me for creating content online. This was in L.A. In my Connecticut kitchen my eyes were barely open in the morning when I saw a video text from my client. It was Gary talking to me! That morning was as much of a frenzy as any, getting my sons to school, but I had made contact with someone who had ten million followers on Instagram. It also felt unbelievable because there I was, a work-from-home Gen Xer mom, communicating with an entrepreneur whose core audience is twelve and male. This is how I jumped to the front of the line while mommying. I told people I was going for something big and I was showcasing in public how little I knew then about landing high-profile podcasting guests. There are some behind-the-scenes moments still out there. I wasn't pretending to be a guru. I was telling people I was new at podcasting and it was GaryVee's fault in a cheeky way.

Lisa admitted that in being up-front about her lack of experience, she hoped people would help her, which they did. For that she's extremely grateful. This strategy has proven effective over and over again. As Lisa says:

> I think we can't underestimate how much it means when people open up their little black book, and they give us a connection, which otherwise could take us years to try and find. Never underestimate the power of being grateful and thankful for contacts and connections.

If you feel a lack of confidence, to take a chance on an idea or think your success is only due to luck, you aren't alone. Many moms feel like impostors in many aspects of their lives but they don't talk about it. Keeping our fears to ourselves is one strategy. However, it might not be good for business or it may impede your trying something new. Lisa managed to build an empire, in an industry that's perceived to be on its last legs, by doing the exact opposite. She used her lack of experience as an asset. It made it possible to ask for all kinds of help, from the creation of her product to entering into conversations with icons, such as former Editor-in-Chief of *Vogue* Dame Anna Wintour. If you are like many moms, chances are you want to use your imagination to bring an idea to the world. So many of us have sparks of business ideas. If you think you can make something better to sell, then Lisa offers you a road map for how to launch or grow an idea and turn your impostor syndrome into an asset. I love that Lisa made that choice, and several other decisions in that vein have contributed to her success. Some of us would die for her lifestyle of travel, but for others it sounds exhausting, especially with kids. The creative-thinking entrepreneurs (e.g., coaches, consultants, podcasters, writers, thought leaders, etc.) I've coached have opted for maximum flexibility. So, what if you could design your career or ambitions in such a way as to support the lifestyle of your dreams? Most of us do the opposite. We add our career or responsibilities to our calendars and try to fit in our lifestyle around them. What follows is a co-owner of a family business who has made choices suitable to the lifestyle that he and his partner desire. Not all of the choices are obvious, especially when it comes to the business of grilling. Think about what you want your life to look like and then see how you can make things work around your own nonnegotiables. Let's look at Chad's story next.

Your turn to take what you've learned in this chapter to play with your imagination. Use the following section to tailor the lessons you've uncovered from this chapter to fuel your imagination this week.

BIG IDEAS

- Use impostor syndrome as an asset by telling others you feel it
- People want to help you; people especially want to help moms, or so I've found
- Seek feedback before it's ready
- Don't waste time writing a perfect business plan; it's not how entrepreneurship works
- Be grateful for those who accelerate your goals

IMAGINATION WARM-UPS

1. Imagine your loftiest vision as related to one individual dream you may have uncovered via this book or that has been on your back burner due to feeling like an impostor.

2. How might not having enough experience be an advantage? Imagine some ways bringing a fresh perspective could be a better thing as related to that dream.

3. Imagine everything you may need to have or know to execute on that vision. What are those items?

4. What key relationships could you imagine being advantageous to you given the things you may need to have or know to pursue your vision?

5. Plan your idea reveal. What do you imagine writing in your editor's note? How will you articulate your inexperience with the world?

Chapter 16

DESIGN YOUR LIFESTYLE

-CHAD ROMZEK, A CO-OWNER OF KICK ASH BASKET®

In this chapter you will:

- Debunk the myth that working can't be fun

- Consider if your current goals or business are imprisoning you

- Design your life on your terms so that it aligns with your priorities

- Start to think about how you can get the most from life for both family and yourself

- See that it is possible to get what you want especially when you invest in an accountability partner to get you to the finish line; it was essential for me in completing this very book

LET'S TALK ABOUT IMPLEMENTATION. Once you've uncovered your dream then how you bring it to life is entirely up to you. Coaches swear by different methods. The permutations of how you could make your dream a reality are endless. We often get stuck thinking there is only one way to deliver our services. This book is about using your imagination. You have preferences. Use them to inform how you want to experience life. Once you've disassembled your mom script, it's time to reassemble it on your terms. You may not have thought to ask for the new parts. So many moms limit their thinking to careers such as teaching so that their schedule coincides with their kids'. Hey, I'm grateful for teachers, especially those who use their imaginations to bring classroom topics alive or to find alternative ways to teach kids with different abilities. I simply want to share that there are so many new ways to contribute. The Internet changed that twenty years ago. You may assume that someone with an idea for grill parts has to open up a grill store, but what if there are other options with greater flexibility?

What if you wanted to develop an idea or launch a business with the intention of supporting your ideal lifestyle? My podcast guests and I have given you lots of ideas on how to work out what that might look like and how to find the energy. It's time to play with your imagination, by taking up that challenge: how can you work to live, not the other way around? What if sleeping peacefully or having more flexibility was important to you? What if it could drive your business-building or idea-conceiving? Sadly, I think the opposite tends to happen. Many founders and creators build something and squeeze living around it. Just to make it through the days and nights of constant work it is no surprise that some resort to microdosing to cope. All of this could be gross stereotypes from the start-up world, but somehow realistic. For example, I know a mom who runs a company valued at over a billion dollars, and I greatly admire her. I can imagine that I would need to skip some daytime school events for my sons, which I love to go to, to pursue what my billion-dollar mom hero feels deeply called to do. If I were planning to found a company that I wanted to sell for over a billion dollars then I imagine I would be chained to my desk. I wouldn't feel free to make time to pee because of the pressure I'd feel from outside investors. However, this is a challenge that is ripe for your imagination to solve if this is your ambition. **Aim to figure out how to work to live (instead of living to work) and you'll surely shake your imagination out of slumber.**

A lot of people have strong opinions about Tony Robbins. He is a results-driven mega coach, in my book, even though he doesn't like to be called a coach. With a Rolodex that I wish I could have, he's coached Mother Teresa and President Clinton. When I saw his documentary, *I'm Not Your Guru*, I was smitten by the rapid turnarounds he produced in his audience members. Some people had been suffering with trauma and addictions for decades yet through Tony's unorthodox coaching he was able to help them transform. That, combined with his zest for life, drew me to him. As a Christmas gift, my husband sent me to Tony's Business Mastery seminar for five days in Fort Lauderdale. This gift, while a privilege, made me hold myself accountable to getting a return on that investment. Having skin in the game motivates me. How about you?

The experience was like nothing I had ever experienced, as a mom with three kids. Maybe my standards are low, but five nights alone in a hotel room was worth the price of admission. Put it this way: I never made my bed. I woke up and ran to the gym. Zero thoughts were spent on feeding anyone, including myself! They gave us food. The event itself was high voltage. I had never seen so many entrepreneurs high on life! Literally, we were jumping out of our seats and screaming like some high schoolers with zero obligations. Mom or dad nirvana. This is where I met Chad Romzek, the inventor of the Kick Ash Basket®, who had brought his love of engineering to the grilling world. It is through Chad's story that you too will have practical ways to use your own imagination playfully to help you build out your big idea on your terms. The "on your terms" part is the area where you can really use your imagination. This distinction will feel like the hardest part.

Chad had worked for two Fortune 500 companies and a start-up before embarking on a side hustle in the barbecue grilling industry. He and his wife, Tracy, started the Kick Ash Basket® business in 2014, from their garage in Wisconsin. They're now supplying grill accessories all over the U.S. and the "Kick Ash Planet." By 2017, as the company continued to grow and bring in consistent sales, Chad was able to walk away from his full-time job. Now Chad and Tracy are kicking ash and making flames with annual sales over seven figures. Chad's life goal is to inspire people all over the world to "Shake that Ash and Light that Fire."

Chad is a dad but sees his primary obligation to his family as ensuring their financial health. In my life, my obligations are different, they relate to the quality of my family's life. It's as if everything other than money has to be on my mind 24/7. Maybe you can relate if you aren't the breadwinner in your home? It's because of this sense of responsibility that I have at times felt resistant to add the burden of making money to my already stuffed plate. It is complicated to make room for this responsibility in my inherited "mom script." My original script read that being an ambitious working mom would lead to failing at my main job: of being a mom. That was my initial read of the script, when my imagination was offline. My fertile imagination has rewritten those lines to say that I can be creative enough to find ways to succeed at my main job of being a mom through the pursuits of my ambitions. It's also okay to smartly invest in myself; it's a need for me. I've heard from many moms that they won't spend money on themselves because they feel their needs are not worth taking money from their kids' college funds. I totally get it, yet there are other ways to define your needs that are worth investing in.

Back to Chad, I once thought that I'd have to sacrifice my nights and days to launch or sustain a business, that I wouldn't be able to help my kids when they needed me. Chad didn't have to make those sacrifices. We reconnected after the Tony Robbins seminar when I saw his family photos on Facebook. They showed this epic mountain bike circuit he'd built on his property. Chad was doing a lot of living, so that got me curious: what might Chad be up to now that he left Kimberly Clark to focus on his grilling business? Those mountain bike circuit pictures clued me into Chad's lifestyle priorities: it's all about his freedoms.

This is what Chad had to say about this ideal way of running a business and those freedoms to be able to spend a working day building a masterful mountain bike course in his yard:

In the age of being able to start a website or a Facebook page to start selling products it made a lot more sense to me to do that than to open up a barbecue shop at the time. Folks still ask me today if I can open up a barbecue shop. I'm like, no, I'll take my freedoms. I like to be able to go out and build mountain bike trails during the days. We get our shipping done in the mornings and then we can kind of do what we want to do. I guess it's a different mindset on the business and on how to look at it. You have to know what you're really committed to [by way of your lifestyle needs] so that you can think about where you want to be down the road in life.

It's easy to be consumed by going big or feeling pressure to do things the way they have been done in the past. Overwhelm is a common feeling once you start to play with your imagination. So it's important for you to decide up front whether you want to retain your freedoms or exchange them right now for your dreams. Imagine how much pressure you will be able to take at your current life stage. What's feasible today? Understand that you can design your business or idea so that it fits in with how you want to feel emotionally.

For example, imagine launching an idea and not freaking out when you put your head on your pillow because of the risks you're taking. Tony Robbins, during his seminar, does talk about burning your boat (i.e., going all in without a safety net) and setting out into the sea of entrepreneurship. He appealed to our sense of adventure. He wanted to inspire us to make big moves and be in a state of excitement and follow through with our inspirations. Some of the audience had already sacrificed a lot just to buy their tickets and so in the spirit of what's another risk, I am sure they ultimately did leave that event deciding to quit their jobs and launch something bigger or better. Meanwhile, some of us wanted to let our business ideas simmer a little longer. This was the case for Chad. It sounds scary to quit a job and then take a leap into an untested business idea. There are plenty of moms who are the breadwinners and that kind of pressure can take some of us to the hospital! Tony's suggestions during that business seminar were not for everyone but that doesn't mean to cross off your dreams. There are other ways to eat this elephant (which is a popular phrase amongst entrepreneurs).

Chad teaches us to start "smart and small"…again, leading with the idea that you get to choose how risky you'd like to be:

> I started my own little business in our home. We shipped out of our garage. We still ship out of our garage. Now, I do have some warehouse space

where I store a little bit more. I think the big thing
is to just take on small chunks that you can manage
and that allow you to sleep at night.

Use your imagination to respond to the following question.
How can I achieve my dream lifestyle and stay true to what
being a mom means to me? If you ever need to kick-start your
imagination, ask yourself a seemingly impossible question
like that one. You are giving your imagination a riddle when
you are making audacious requests; playing lets you come up
with more fertile ideas. Your imagination will come to your
rescue because it is like a mom who hates seeing dirty dishes
at the end of her day. Your imagination gets frustrated when
a challenge remains unsolved. Mine has felt restless at times
in this very way. So it is at this point, once you've riled up
your imagination, that you can use it to think about your
desired lifestyle. What do you need to feel comfortable about
launching a business, writing a book, or putting yourself out
there in your zone of genius? Imagine for a moment your
sanity. What would help you sleep peacefully at night? Six
months of a cash runway or health insurance may be critical
to you. Your need does not have to be the same as everyone
else's. Ask yourself: what would worry me? Then how can
I mitigate that risk? Ask your imagination to help you out.
We've covered this, in Gabriele's chapter; hopefully your
imagination is already working on it.

Do you think you need formal training for anything you desire? I would disagree. As an MBA-graduate, who was extensively trained in theories, I have come to realize that the only way to win outside of a corporate environment is to have the guts to go first and have a bias for action. Experience is the best training. Will your idea work? Does anyone want it? You can overthink this in your head as much as you'd like but unless you launch (or test in market) something you won't really know whether something is worth your time and effort. Chad even goes so far as to say this about his schooling experience:

> I took an entrepreneurial class at our local college. You'll learn a lot about writing business plans. You'll get into the nitty-gritty before you even know if you've got something you can sell. And quite honestly, it probably set me back a year. It might have been 2010/2011 or something like that. Really what helped kick us off is working with our business coach again, and saying, "Hey, how do we just take a small chunk? What can we do and see if we've got a good idea?"

Chad's idea gained the most traction when he hired a Tony Robbins coach. This coach wasn't focused on business frameworks. He was asking great questions to make the business-building process feel totally doable in simple action steps. His coach suffocated Chad's feeling of being overwhelmed. You'll want to skip the overwhelm and focus on micro steps too. This is what Chad realized out of the coaching engagement.

So many people that I talk to get analysis paralysis. Instead, ask yourself: what are the three things that you need to do this week? To move you forward? When you get somebody to whom you're paying a good amount of money to ask you these questions, like my coach, you say to yourself: okay, I'm going to get it done. The other thing is that a coach is your accountability partner. I was preparing notes to send him so he could review them before our meeting. He was keeping me on top of it all. He'd ask me: "what do we have going on? What's next? Did we do what we said we're going to do?" We'd also talk about hard discussions. We have to have...with suppliers and manufacturers or whomever. Did we follow through on that? It's not any one thing but it's like: "hey, what do you want to do?" So, questions including this one: "what's holding you back?"

It's time to play with your imagination. Use some of the strategies in my other chapters such as the one with our resident decision engineer Michelle Florendo or Gabriele Corcos, who followed his passions. Who can you ask to be your accountability partner? I have been an accountability partner for so many professionals and entrepreneurs who seek motivating solutions. All successful people ask for help.

We're told it takes a village to raise a child. What if we applied this "village thinking" to helping ourselves live out our dreams? Imagine your personal dream team or kitchen cabinet. These people can help you not only build your dream but also hold you accountable for doing so. I told my clients I was launching a podcast. I was talking to them every week. For me, revealing my action steps to building my podcast meant that I would be disappointing all of us if I didn't take them. When you tell people your goals, they'll begin to feel invested in them too! In my coaching practice, I've seen massive changes in behavior in moms specifically when their activities were tracked on a visible dashboard for all of us to see. Meanwhile, as a mom of three sons, mom excuses were often off the table and progress was made possible through the use of the group's fertile imaginations. What about you?

So now that you are using your imagination to build something that fits your ideal lifestyle and then figuring out who can hold you accountable, it's now time to use your imagination to find other resources. In my case, the resource I needed, to launch my podcast, was someone who had done it before. What if you brought your dreams everywhere you went and started telling everyone what you needed?

Chad's wife did just that. Tracy is an engineer too but this was her being a mom and that's how they began their online presence.

> We found our website guy in an unexpected place. Tracy ran into him at a farmer's market in town here in Neenah, Wisconsin. She struck up a conversation with him. It turns out that he had a website development company as another part of his business. That's how we met him. We wanted to start with a simple, smart website. He, to this day, still tells that story, because he sees so many people who have this great idea, haven't sold a thing yet, who want to spend $15,000 on a website. He uses our story of starting with $5,000, which is not a drop in the bucket but very, very smart, very conservative, and just running with it from there.

As moms, we often undervalue our networks. I've sat in soccer meetups and rubbed elbows with moms and dads who had impressive careers. Plan to get to know more about the people around you. It's of value. Guess what? You may also be the missing link for someone else. Another mom might need your copywriting skills. Don't hide your dreams. Add them to your pocketbook just like everything else we tend to carry along with us. Look for help. Ask for help. Challenge yourself today. Go to the supermarket. Ask your imagination: *how can I find my executive assistant in here?* Questions will wake up your imagination. They make for a fertile ground on which to play out a ton of possibilities. They always do for me.

In the case of Chad and Tracy, they wanted to build a fun company. Would you want the same? Ultimately, when you play with your imagination, seeking fun will be a by-product. Grilling is supposed to be fun. This is how Chad and Tracy managed to use their imagination to bring this top of mind.

> Our company culture is fun. We're helping people make food for their family and friends. We're going to keep it light and fun. We mess stuff up. Don't get me wrong. Whatever Tracy and I can do to put systems in place and optimize our shipping or bookkeeping [we do]. We have a CPA who helps us out. Tracy still kind of gets overwhelmed with some of the shipping stuff and even customer

calls. But if we share customer calls that's part of the fun too. We're talking to people from all over the country, all over the world, about their grill. So it's good fun. I'd say our business culture is just good fun.

Is it hard to imagine figuring out how to build a business or think about your creative endeavor in a way that aligns with keeping your freedoms, having fun, and sleeping peacefully at night? Chad and Tracy managed to do this and so can you. It requires an imagination because the alternative narrative is draining. Chad left corporate with a creative idea already set in motion. What if you've been working for some time and have no idea what life without a traditional career can look like? What might be possible if you are experiencing emotional ups and downs and just can't make yourself come up with a creative business idea that would excite you? Any way you can include your kids and have them coach you on using your imagination? Jo Dodd worked for decades in a leadership role for a big brand. She had always felt there must be more out there for her but the corporate grind made it hard to see beyond the fog. Want to hear how Jo played with her imagination? That's up next!

Your turn to take what you've learned in this chapter to play with your imagination. Use the following section to tailor the lessons you've uncovered from this chapter to fuel your imagination this week.

BIG IDEAS

- Question conventional approaches to achieving your goal
- Design your lifestyle and then insert your work
- Hire a coach to hold you accountable
- You don't have to burn your boat and make yourself stressed out
- Find ways to conservatively take a risk or explore the viability of an idea

IMAGINATION WARM-UPS

1. Imagine your ideal lifestyle. Can you describe it in detail?

2. What would an ideal day look like for you and your family in the context of your dreams?

3. Imagine having your cake and eating it too. Where would you want to do your business or create?

4. What's one company value that you'd love to live?

5. Can you imagine for two minutes your dream team? Who would make for great accountability partners?

Chapter 17

INVOLVE YOUR KID'S IMAGINATION

-JO DODD, THE AUTHOR OF *DEAR MAMA BEAR WITH THE F'CKED UP HAIR*

In this chapter you will:

- Stop and ask yourself: Am I okay?
- Relate to the story of a mom who felt out of balance and wanted more
- See how taking a break can help you consider alternatives
- Open your imagination by engaging with your kids
- Witness how a corporate high flyer re-created her life by embracing her mom identity

MY SONS PLAY a role in my business. I may not have given them job titles, but I consult with them if things have gotten too complicated to unravel by myself. My sons paint masterfully (says every mom, right?). Well, my boys have adorned my living room with works of art featuring the most colorful Super Mario goombas. They get lost in painting, especially my eldest, always seeing life in video game pixels. I wanted their help so I bought an extra canvas and begged them to paint a masterpiece. I asked them to paint something that would remind me to use my imagination, make sure it reminds me I am creative. My youngest decided to make it his own. The final result is half red and half white. In reality, I prefer their goombas, but as the person who commissioned the piece, it met my specs. I see it every morning next to the sink and before I close the kitchen for the night. Seeing their paintings hanging in our kitchen makes my little artists feel special too. We have these kids. They are imaginative. Why not use their talents to amplify our own?

If you've ever felt conflicted about work and motherhood then this is the chapter for you. This is an opportunity to see how other moms have untangled this inner dialogue. Your mortgage might make some choices impossible for you. It's still important to look at what might be under the hood if you have a gnawing feeling that there might be more out there for you.

Sometimes, as moms, we think we are invincible. We take on more and more without even realizing we are overwhelmed. During one of my weekly team meetings as a young marketing analyst at American Express (AmEx) I witnessed a vice president, who was a mom, at her breaking point. It was a light bulb moment for me. I had never seen an executive cry in front of her team before. I thought I was just there to learn about that week's set of priorities when our VP announced that after having her second child she would leave AmEx. It didn't add up for me. In my pre-mom mind I thought she had it all. She had a Stern MBA and became a VP when many moms at AmEx were stuck at the director level. But she had come to the conclusion that she wanted to embrace her new role as a mom and was, I imagine, crying because she was relieved but also grieving over her decision to walk away from the corporate ladder. I wondered what her plan was at the time; later on she decided to become a freelancer for AmEx. In 2004, before being able to dial into the office with Skype and Zoom, it took an imagination to create a flexible role like she did. Somehow she was able to create a way to use her skills and avoid having the stress of a business leader with profit-loss responsibilities, politics, and climbing a corporate ladder. That moment stuck with me. Her resignation was powerful.

As I reflect on that moment I wonder how it informed the careers of the other women in that meeting.

In my opinion, she didn't leave because she couldn't handle the corporate pressure, instead what I saw was a woman who chose to bring her leadership skills to her family. That felt so badass at the time. It's such a huge decision to make. What about in your life? Are there any mom trailblazers for you?

Another ambitious woman who figured out how to embrace her motherhood identity after leaving a leadership role in her corporate career is Jo Dodd. In Jo's case, not only did she decide to use her leadership skills full-time for her family, she also figured out how to enlist the help of her kids to play with her imagination. Over a period of twenty-five years Jo worked in various roles for a Fortune 500 company. She is a mom to four boys, the youngest of whom has a learning disability. When she was furloughed during the pandemic; she decided to step away from her leadership role. She created Jotopia Productions LLC, her own coaching, publishing company where she gets to live her own utopic life as a present mom. So far she has published four books, including an illustrated book for moms called *Dear Mama Bear with the F*cked Up Hair,* and cowritten a book with Joseph, her youngest son, called *We All Like Different Things and That's A-OK With Me.*

What struck me as surprising was how Jo was unable to see the possibilities available to her while she was in the corporate world. Jo hadn't realized, all those years in the rat race, she had been running on empty. You end up on empty because success is addictive. Biweekly paychecks are like heroin. Pair these attractions with corporate expectations and it's no wonder people aren't dropping on the floor after a huge presentation more often. **Turns out you need to be running on full to let your creativity bubble up to the top. You may have something creative that your kids can help you with.**

However while she was in the corporate world, Jo did know:

> I wanted more for my life. I knew that I wasn't supposed to be doing this role in Corporate America and just couldn't return to it. Like you said, that heroin hit, that paycheck and oh, the next promotion and looking for the next job. I knew that was draining me. But at the same time, I was so addicted to that and so terrified of what was outside of that, I couldn't see it. It's almost like you don't want to stop, you don't want to slow down for fear of the fact that you're going to have maybe a breakdown. The scary part is saying, No, I'm not okay, but what's next?

This was a huge insight; it never occurred to me that what I was seeing as pain and suffering in a lot of working moms could be invisible to the mom herself. A lot of us are walking around immersed in the rat race or operating at a fast pace with all sorts of undone healing. In Jo's case not knowing what was next was scary. I'm sure it was the same for that VP at AmEx. Is it for you? Regardless of whether you are contemplating making a big career or life change? It turns out that "what's next" couldn't surface to the top for Jo when she was running on empty at work. If you are nervous about an upcoming change and the nerves are due to not knowing what life is going to look like next for you then you may need to check if you are running on empty...this goes for stay-at-home moms too.

This is how Jo experienced this:

> I didn't know how to relax because that was so foreign to me as a working mum. What do I do now, the job part has suddenly gone away? It took a good couple of weeks to settle into: wow, this is kind of nice, even though I had the worries of the finances and all of that, I sort of just let that go. I just knew it would take care of itself. I don't know why I didn't worry. I was probably in denial. I just sort of sunk into this world where I felt safe not having work in the corporate world anymore. And that's when all this creativity started coming out of me.

You might be running on empty and not even know. This was the case for Jo, who helped me see that sometimes my clients may have actually been blind to their pain; it wasn't even denial. Do you know how many nights I spent utterly confused if I was going nuts and imagining that working moms were on the brink of breaking? And in those cases, the moms would tell me they were okay or just loved a little drama?

So again, what about those of you who are not in a corporate rat race? When Jo left corporate, she realized that this need to keep doing and overworking yourself is tough to shake and it's a mindset more than a matter of a setting.

What Jo went on to share with me is that even when she left corporate, she continued to maintain a hectic schedule.

In Jo's words:

> Things were starting to tick along and then my oldest son, who's twenty-five, had a nervous breakdown. It brought me to my knees. I was trying to run my own business, trying to be a mum to three other boys, and then trying to figure out how I could help my twenty-five-year-old. It was just too much because, again, I'd been running

on empty for so long. I'd stepped away from the corporate world and felt this massive release. But then I hadn't really stepped away from that mentality, I was still thinking like, I have to work hard, I have to work hard, I have to work hard. And so I was just taking that corporate mentality and applying it to my business.

So here's what you and I need to do, let's check in to see if we might be blocking our own flow of imagination.

Jo suggests...

The first step is to really look at yourself in the mirror. Just look, give yourself a minute and don't look away, then ask yourself, "Am I okay?" Be silent and ask again, "Am I okay?" And if there are tears that come, then you're probably not. You may notice a resistance in your body, it might feel really uncomfortable. It's the weirdest thing to do, but once you do it, it opens something up inside. When you admit to yourself that you're not okay, that's the first step in your healing journey. Again, it's the weirdest thing to do, but I actually do it a lot now.

Jo applies this all the time in her life. She even shares with her sons the moments when she is not okay. So whatever you are doing, in pursuit of goals that might no longer serve you, just take a second to stop and do this exercise. When Mommy is good then her cubs have a chance to be good too. Otherwise, everyone can suffer.

After you get into a good place through therapy, meds, support, whatever is right for you, ask yourself, how do I want to live my life? What ways can I integrate my kids into my hopes and dreams? How can we fulfill our greatness, side by side? The changing needs of our kids as they grow and develop bring continual challenges. Your needs change too. So ensuring both you and your kids have what they need, from attention to inspiration and support, means you must be a family barometer. Did you know that? You are the barometer of your family. Checking to see if you are overheating is important for everyone's well-being, not just yours.

Jo hired her sons to help ensure her imagination stays awake and ready to play. Isn't it interesting how we have these little imagination experts around us but seldom do we leverage their superpower for our own dreams?

At first I gave them roles. So Ethan, my now twelve-year-old, was my Director of Dreams because he would not let me dream small. I had to dream big with him. I love that about him. That innocence, you can go off to do anything, you can have whatever you want. Then my youngest, Joseph, is my Director of Bear Hugs and Belly Laughs, because who doesn't need bear hugs and belly laughs in their life, and what a great position to have. So they were heavily involved, I shared everything with them. I shared the struggle, the fear, and the celebration!

How can you give your kid(s) roles to help keep your imagination alive? Think about it this way: you are borrowing from the childhood game of role-playing to bond. What are some ways you can enroll them in your dreams? What working solution fits your desires and how you want to show up as a mom? You get to intentionally rewrite your mom script all the time. Once we prioritize our imagination and get reacquainted with its capabilities we can pass the baton to our kids. Really pass the baton, so they feel emboldened, ready and able to run whatever race they desire. Jo doesn't just write books and give her kids job titles. Jo's son got to write a book himself as an apprentice to his mom. This is more powerful and potent than to hear his mom cheerlead him on from the sidelines. In this case, both mom and son are invested in the creations of each other's imagination. This is what the world needs more of.

> Joseph had watched a movie, *Trolls World Tour*. We were just having this amazing conversation about how it's okay that everybody likes different things when he came up with this phrase—"We all like different things." Then he said, "that's okay with me," and I was like, that's a book, you know. So we wrote a book. I wrote a poem, he then helped me tweak it so it sounded right for him. It's about Joseph thinking about our family, how different we are and how we all like different things, and then extending that to the bigger world to how everybody's different and everybody likes something different. It was great just to watch him, he has learning disabilities, he has some real struggles especially with reading and writing, but to watch his confidence grow was awesome. We launched the book with a book launch party, where he was signing copies. To see him doing that was so rewarding. I thought, I don't care how many copies this book sells, he'll always remember this, I'll always remember this. Watching his confidence just bloom and blossom was something I'll never forget.

This is what's possible when a mom decides to prioritize finding a way to see the greatness in herself. It makes it impossible for our kids to forget what's so great about themselves. It's important to check if your tank is full or empty so that your imagination has a shot at giving you a path to a new future. Jo's idea of looking at ourselves in the mirror is an easy way we can do this every day. It's important that we check in with ourselves especially when we are busiest. Your fear of what might come next might indicate that you really need to bravely take a moment for some honest self-reflection for the sake of yourself and your kids. Once you are full it is then that your imagination will reawaken and your kids will be able to help you keep it in use together. Playing is your imagination in use.

At this point, you should have some ideas of how to merge your priorities in a way that feels natural. As you work on your creative outlet, will you be motivated to do it for both you and for your kids? Playing with your imagination is a never-ending endeavor. After reading this chapter you should become more nimble; exposing yourself to interests and ideas that might have felt foreign to you before. It's time to take your reawakened imagination that you've been playing with and, by engaging with others, really stretch out this superpower to its max. What if we could sustain this practice of using our imagination and enlisting the help of others to keep us honest and truly challenging ourselves?

In the next section, we will explore how to stretch the imagination you have just awoken. It will give you tools to help you pursue the impact you wish to make with the help of your new fertile imagination.

Your turn to take what you've learned in this chapter to play with your imagination. Use the following section to tailor the lessons you've uncovered from this chapter to fuel your imagination this week.

BIG IDEAS

- Check in with yourself especially when you are the busiest
- Kids enjoy being involved in what lights us up
- Survival mode clogs up your creative juices so get out of there whenever possible
- Busy is a mindset, not something a boss makes us be
- Integrating being a mom and businessperson (or anything else) is doable

IMAGINATION WARM-UPS

1. Imagine a typical day in your life. What moments have felt like a struggle lately that you'd like to make more pleasant?

2. When you did that mirror exercise how did you feel? If you didn't, then try now.

3. Imagine two or three ways you can refill your tank.

4. Imagine all the help your kid(s) can provide. What job titles would you give them?

5. What might be some co-creations you can do with your kid(s) to bring out the imagination in each of you?

III.

STRETCH YOUR IMAGINATION

BY NOW YOU should be bouncing with excitement and energy. It's time to build a plan of action. In this section, I want you to stretch your imagination beyond recognition. Imagine if you learned how to optimize your fertile imagination for maximum impact? Consider the range of fertile ideas that could be available to you. What if, through your actions, you could be the wake-up call other moms need? Anything is possible! You'll need internal and external resources you can count on during the various seasons of mom life. Taking a fertile idea to the finish line during busy seasons or in between them requires skipping steps whenever possible and being nimble to stay the course. The same is true about making mom jeans look cute—some days you'll be thankful you got a pair that can stretch enough to button them up. Whatever it takes, right? In this section, I will share one method you can use, at the drop of a dime, as you pursue the interests that light you up. Next you'll read how the Socratic method can save you a decade of going in the wrong direction. I'll encourage you to enlist people who know you and will call BS if you aren't doing nearly as much as what you are capable of.

This concept of stretching your imagination requires a change of mindset and asking others for help. You'll feel confident changing your mind and reframing your relationship with money. While this book includes oodles of my personal stories and the stories of my podcast guests, I want to be sure that you understand that your story matters too. You might be the missing piece that can complete someone else's puzzle. Wouldn't that be amazing? Let's close this section with how we began, in bringing back our inner little girl. She may have been through a lot and even lost her ability to wake up, play with, and stretch her imagination because life threw things her way that caused her to stop imagining dreams for herself. It's time to rewrite your mom script. Ready to stretch your imagination? Let's go.

If you haven't yet visited my website for the downloadable Imagination Warm-Ups then be sure to do so. It's important to have extra space to document as many ideas as possible on how to apply the wisdom in this book to your own life. Do you wonder if after playing with your imagination your quiz results have changed? Take the free quiz on my website to check your Imagination Wellness Assessment. It's important to know where to pour your finite energy and best creative-thinking to pursue bigger entrepreneurial dreams. You'll also find the original podcast interviews featured in this section, coaching offers to further stretch your imagination, and my latest updates at:

www.fertileideas.com

Most importantly, you'll also want to join the **Imagination to Impact Five-Day Challenge** (valued at $49, yours for free) to reawaken, play with, and stretch your imagination to discover your most fertile idea. This is where to start to experience firsthand what using your fertile imagination can look like in your daily life with your kids.

Chapter 18

PAUSE AND ASK YOURSELF QUESTIONS

-MARC CHAMPAGNE, THE AUTHOR OF *PERSONAL SOCRATES*

In this chapter you will:

- See the value of pausing intentionally every single day

- Use self-reflective questions to spare yourself a decade of going in the wrong direction

- Always double-check you are doing something fruitful and related to your dreams

- Address the constant barrage of interruptions around us

- Discover the technical hack to help you navigate all the constant interruptions we experience

IS IT ONLY ME, or have you ever felt like your head was not in the game because perhaps your kid got sick and you had to change your plans or something unexpected and emotionally draining threw you off from having a nearly perfect day? If, as a primary caregiver, you can apply the tool you will learn about in this chapter to your daily life then you will achieve your goal—whether it's to get through this book or to write your own. I'm going to introduce you to the Socratic method of stopping and asking yourself questions. I'm going to show you how to use these pauses to your advantage.

According to my "mom script," being the primary caregiver means that anything I want to pursue must get done around the big and small needs of those I care for. When given the choice to write my manuscript or wipe boogers out of my youngest's nose, I will always run with my tissue ready to go! The slippery slope is that kids need a lot of things. If I listened to that "mom script" then I wouldn't get anything done for myself. Sometimes this takes self-restraint. Nose wiping is a quick payoff. My book on the other hand is a sluggish endeavor and not my top priority according to my "mom script." Many parents who are not the primary caregivers do not have the same pull to scoop out snots. However, if you don't proactively manage these primary caregiver interruptions then you will find yourself wishing you could pull out someone's green slime in eighteen years because you set aside your personal interests for so long.

I have felt frazzled and frustrated before school, every single morning for over a decade trying to feed breakfast to my picky eaters. I have gone as far as outsourcing feeding them because the morning explosions shot my nerves. If I knew what it took to feed one child I think I wouldn't have had them: it's THAT bad in my house. Except, of course, when we order french fries; somehow the floodgates open for junk food.

I thought I could brush off this feeling of being frazzled and frustrated. I'd just force myself to pound my laptop while in that mental state. I assumed the craziness wouldn't affect my business or my brain if I ignored it. I've come to realize I was carrying enormous annoyance and resentment into my business every single day. The annoyance was having to do Jedi tricks to feed my sons and the resentment was from putting out so much online content that didn't gain any traction. When you compound that with the frustrations that come from learning new technology, as well as trying to overcome typical business challenges, it wears me down. It's also led me to show up at times with no patience for anyone who adds to my angst. Even a disgruntled prospective client who seeks my coaching but runs from its price. Showing up to my laptop, without a pause, has sometimes brought out the worst in me, resulting in some poor choices.

If you don't learn to pause and reflect, then new thoughts and ideas are just more knowledge filling your mind library, right? Which is okay because it's there. But odds are, we're probably not going to go explore and pull it off the shelf.

A pause is essential to gain clarity, on where you are now and where you stand in relation to your future goals, especially for moms. Mom life, at least for me, has been a daily battle for mental clarity. These past years have felt like one unexpected tornado behind another that could have lifted me off-course of my ambitions. We live and breathe a life of interruptions, so how can we set ourselves up to achieve our most imaginative goals?

Marc Champagne loves the art of asking questions as much as I do. He wrote a book called *Personal Socrates*; in it he draws on interviews with award-winning writers, designers, photographers, strategists, entrepreneurs, technologists, musicians, athletes, and more to provide inspiration and examples as to where and how pointed self-inquiry can help your health, happiness, and performance.

Marc has been in the mental fitness business for over a decade and he has picked up on the key to our ultimate success. He says:

> [To achieve big goals takes] being consistent and focused on putting the right actions forward or taking the right steps.

This reads like the total opposite of being a mom. We are constantly flying by the seat of our pants and adjusting all the time. What I have also realized is the constant interruptions can draw us in the opposite direction of where we want to be. If we don't force ourselves to take a pause, even for just ten minutes, they can lead us astray. Often, we are busiest when we are in survival mode, navigating daily interruptions and our usual mom duties. Take this familiar reality that I've noticed around the world, from the U.S. to Australia—our collective morning routines of trying to get our kids off to school.

Marc describes it like this:

> When you wake up and you're feeling fogged or stressed or something's bothering you, there are two things that can be done. You can just plow through and step into the day pulling all of that tension with you. Which makes it really hard to do your best thinking, do your best work, right? You're kind of in that survival state. There's fear, there's anxiety, you're just not feeling on the top of your game.

So what does Marc suggest instead?

> Or, you can take a microsecond—a micro pause—
> while you're preparing your tea or your coffee is
> brewing, you're having your first cup of water, and
> check in with yourself, right? Like, how do I feel
> right now? Where do I feel emotion in my body?
> Often just acknowledging where it is, releases it.
> I'm only sharing this because we have to be clear, to
> be able to check in and think, Oh, I'm actually not
> doing the right thing that's going to support the
> objective I have set for today, the month, or for the
> year or whatever legacy I'm building. Whatever it
> is that lights you up, we need those check-ins to
> just spot-check.

I wish I had found Marc years earlier, but I wasn't looking for a solution because I didn't realize I had a problem. A fellow mom did once point it out to me, but I was stubborn and desperate to just get everything done before I had to drop off my twins at preschool. It took me another decade of motherhood until I finally turned the corner and added a daily pause. It may be a twenty-minute meditation, responding to writing prompts, or going to the gym. In Australia, ever since 2020, I didn't have one day where I didn't plan my own pause.

I used this pause to ask myself questions. I'm obsessed with asking myself questions because, by default, they give me the pause I need. After years of interviewing lots of wildly successful humans, I noticed that they're all instinctively using the Socratic method. They'd start with a big question, then they'd ask more questions to unpack it, stimulating critical thinking, drawing out ideas and underlying presuppositions. It was time to try it on myself. I instinctively knew that asking myself reflective questions to uncover a fresh perspective of my business and where I should pour my energy was critical. So when my husband suggested that I pause my business during the pandemic when my emotional bandwidth for my business snapped, I did just that. I was using too much energy making sales calls, receiving over 300 rejections, it made me so resentful and angry. It made me feel on edge and frazzled and I couldn't ignore it anymore. If I was going to be homeschooling my sons, I refused to give them my leftover energy. I didn't want to lose my temper with them because someone in Idaho didn't want to hire me to help them land their "dream" marketing job. I took a pause to reflect on whether my business was working for me anymore. I gave myself the 106 days I spent in lockdown to be introspective. I spent that time asking myself a big question: whom did I want to empower most? Whom would I go to the ends of the Earth to embolden? It felt scary but I inadvertently applied the Socratic method on myself...

Marc asserts that we need to pause to understand if what we are doing daily is going to help us achieve our goals.

In his words:

> We have to first understand, whether it's personally or professionally: are we climbing the right mountain? Right? Who is the person we are right now? Who are we striving to become? Where are we going? Same with our business: we're here, we want to go to this [other] place. We need to understand those two points. Then that's the next step. It's where the focus comes in and where the prompts around intentional thought, or intentional habits and systems, like doing the things that will support the person that we're striving to become or the business that we're trying to build, [come in].

What are your two points? Take ten minutes, or the entire summer break, to ask yourself questions to uncover who you are striving to become. Start by asking: where am I today? And, where do I want to be in the future?

If I hadn't taken that pause, I would still be resentfully pitching to help professionals land full-time jobs and I would not have written this book. My patience would have continued to wear thin. Sure the schools closed and that was historic, but to have kept climbing up the wrong mountain would have pained me; the pandemic just forced me to take a big pause and ask some big questions. When I looked at whom I wanted to empower most and what vehicles made sense for the future me, I thought about moms who were consumed with motherhood and who felt like they lacked a purpose beyond being a mom. The ones who didn't feel like they had something fulfilling going on that powerfully showcased their talents and ambitions. Creative moms who wanted to turn their passion projects into entrepreneurial adventures (e.g., coaching programs, podcasts, books, workshops, etc.) that can create maximum impact. I saw in them an enormous amount of untapped potential, if only they could use their imagination to make life work for them. These were the conversations that excited me most. The vehicles were my podcast and writing this book for moms; this is why checking in with myself transformed my future.

Life continues to throw interruptions. However we've all heard the saying, *you must put your oxygen mask on first before helping others.* So if I don't take those ten minutes every morning, I'm not as good as a mom, as a wife, as a friend, as a partner. At the start of every day I ask myself: What can I do today that is going to get me to where I want to go? Often I have felt that pull to go back to what I know and had worked hard to build. But I need to be consistent and focused on my new future, and you will need to do the same. Once you awaken your imagination you will need to stay the course every step of the way. You will be interrupted. You will feel the inertia of reverting to whatever mom script you've been handed, but by applying a pause into your daily habits and asking yourself questions you can quickly get back on track.

Stretch your imagination and ask yourself reflective questions so you can bring your best thinking to your day. Remember by pausing and asking yourself these questions you will help your state of mind even if it's been a rough morning. This practical insight can make you a better mom, partner, and friend too.

You will be pulled in different directions. You won't get to your goals if you are being ruled by little Machiavellians. Interruptions are part of our lives. You must make sure they don't gobble up too many days. You and I are uniquely pulled in by our kids. They know how to tug at our heartstrings. As a mom we are yanked (sometimes literally) by our kids. You will need to navigate this intentionally. Prioritizing a pause or a couple of them to make sure you are making progress on your non-mom goals will be a lifesaver as it has been for me. While our loved ones can be the cause of these disruptions in our daily lives, there are major benefits if we include them in the loop of our ambitions and interests. We need people who truly know what we are made of, to stretch our imaginations. Coming up is the story of a single mom who encouraged her son to master his craft and to aim higher. You may have seen his work on Showtime. Follow me to the next chapter to hear how having a personal fan can skyrocket your efforts too. Shall we?

Your turn to take what you've learned in this chapter to stretch your imagination. Use the following section to tailor the lessons you've uncovered from this chapter to fuel your imagination this week.

BIG IDEAS

- A one-second pause once a day can save you a decade of going in the wrong direction or none
- Use the gift of questions to uncover what must get done to achieve your goal
- Assume you will be interrupted; plan for it and have tools
- Ensure you have a way to get yourself on track
- Rough morning, nights, lives can derail you without even realizing it

IMAGINATION WARM-UPS

1. Imagine yourself in a decade. What can you imagine having accomplished?

2. Where are you today in relation to that accomplishment?

3. Look at these two points, what's the gap?

4. Can you imagine the two or three daily habits of someone who has achieved your goal?

5. Imagine the best way to check in on your mental state and progress. What tools (alarm bells, Post-it notes, etc.) can you use to remind yourself to ensure you are on track?

Chapter 19

FIND A PERSONAL FAN

-THEO TRAVERS, AN EXECUTIVE PRODUCER OF *BILLIONS*

In this chapter you will:

- Witness how having someone who truly gets you and is invested in seeing you shine, is an invaluable member of your support system

- See how being humble can help you achieve your dreams

- Be reminded that our kids are following our lead

- Realize that artistic pursuits can be learned in the same conventional way as other skills

- Understand how only getting close to your dreams is still not enough

KNOWING THE DIFFERENCE between having the support of a mentor versus the support of someone who knows you intimately is huge. A partner, a parent, or anyone you have let into your life who knows your story will bring a unique perspective to the table. They'll know your strengths and will expect you to bring your best effort. Strangers won't have any context nor will they share your success in the same way with you, truly reaping the rewards of mentorship.

It's my husband who is the president of my fan club and the hopeful dreamer for me. For context, let me tell you how I started my podcast. I was cooking rice and black beans for my family, being the best Cuban granddaughter I could have been in my abuela's eyes, when my husband walked over. He told me about a James Altucher podcast episode, where his guest Gary Vaynerchuk said on record that he wanted the listeners to launch a podcast. Gary went on to say, if someone launched a podcast because of his conversation with James, then he would be their fourth guest. (You may recall that story from another chapter?) James Altucher then jumped in and said, "I'll be your guest too." With some pot burning or another, I felt this gush of "this is a dare" overcome me. It was that moment that I felt like I had to create a podcast. The opportunity to interview two guests, with millions upon millions of listeners, was too huge not to try. As someone who is curious and loves asking people deeply personal, but respectful, questions this was my dream; but it was my husband who opened my mind to it. I'm not the only one with a personal fan club.

Theo Travers was a Tisch student when we first met back in 1997, at New York University. We lived in a dorm building filled with undergraduates who all thought we could become anything. I want to be clear about what anything means in a private institution that teaches film. You know Lady Gaga? She walked the NYU campus. So yes, Tisch students really do believe they could be rocking a meat dress at the Grammys someday. What I didn't know about Theo, when we met in Goddard Hall, was that he was accepted into the top two arts schools in the U.S. I also didn't realize that as a high schooler he'd sent John Singleton a letter asking him for advice about which school to go for. John is best known for the movie *Boyz n the Hood*. Theo saw John's name in the credits as a teen.

This is what Theo has to say about that moment:

> One of the first things that sparked my attention in terms of even pursuing writing as a career was watching *Boyz n the Hood* for maybe the second or third time. Way down deep in the credits, filmmaker John Singleton thanked the USC film writing program. It dawned on me, I was like, you go to school for that? It was the first time, and it

occurred to me. Oh, look at all those names. In the credits, every single one of these people has a career [in writing]. So if you can go to art school and study to become an art designer, if you can go to a music conservatory and learn how to produce and score music, it stands to reason that you could also go to school to learn writing.

But Theo's *mother* had also planted this idea in his head before he watched that movie.

One advantage I had being raised by a mom who's a musician is that I, very early on, was taught the idea that being a specialist is a craft. If you approach your career like a craft, the success that you have with it is a direct correlation to how good you are at your craft.

Theo is the son of a single mom who followed her dream of being a musician, so she is the perfect role model to encourage her son to do the same. This idea of having a personal fan or even a mentor is close to my heart. In my family, there was no one to ask for guidance about achieving my dreams because I had no one who dreamt like me. My dad went to college, so getting into a college was not my highest ambition. My sights were set on getting into the most academically competitive ones. Based on my ambitious goals, I set out to find someone outside of my family (and beyond my cynical high school guidance counselor) who would ultimately become a personal fan. When I was seventeen, I decided to seek a different counselor, in a nonprofit organization called *Aspira*. It was there that I was assigned to Tanya, someone who has since risen to the CEO role in the nonprofit world herself, who took me under her wing during my college application process. It was Tanya who told me to go through one of those huge physical college admissions books and to pick where I wanted to apply. Later, she was the one who told me to apply for many scholarships to fund my prime-rib–priced choices. Maybe she saw herself in me. Either way, she took my school choices seriously and felt like I could get money for college. I recall when we first met, I was impressed that Tanya had earned a partial scholarship to NYU, which was back then a $100K investment. Turns out, I was able to earn a full ride and extra cash because she believed in me and supported me. When I applied to business school years later, I found another personal fan who had what I wanted, an MBA from Wharton. This time it was Kerry who volunteered to guide me through that application process. I never got in. I was waitlisted, which is massive for a girl who is not a quantitative thinker. But, I earned another free ride—this time to Dartmouth. So having personal fans and honoring the wisdom and belief they saw in me helped get the best education my money didn't have to buy.

Theo, at the time of our interview, was an executive producer of the Showtime hit *Billions*. He is a writer living in Hollywood. Your individual dream does not have to be in a creative field nor so cutthroat. It should however make you jump out of your skin if you do eventually make it real. Theo's path was not linear. Although it's an amazing school, you don't get a showrunner job upon graduation from Tisch.

Theo was in a shadow career until his thirties. Shadow careers are essentially those jobs many of us settle for when our dream roles feel impossible to snag. It's like the aspiring landscape artist who works in production for PBS reruns of Bob Ross. I've heard that show business is a young man's career. Making yourself available at the drop of a dime takes energy. This is why the Hollywood scene is filled with waiters, waitresses, and hourly employees. You can't be tied to a fixed schedule. You also can't be in Memphis, Tennessee, and apply from out of state.

Theo was a news anchor then. He had achieved success. While he was living the American Dream, ultimately he had to believe that he was good enough at his craft to work in his dream field. Essentially, Theo needed to have what I didn't have during my early copywriting want-to-be days. He calls it a bit of "self-delusion"; I would call it the desire to be truly great at your craft, so much so that you are willing to humble yourself. The idea of humbling yourself can help a mom feel free to explore new ideas. **The thinking "I should know this or be further along" has stopped many people from uncovering their purpose or making progress toward their dreams.** Has this thought ever stopped you from starting something? It can be embarrassing to stumble your way into learning a new craft, but this is what we are watching our kids do at every stage (why not join them and be their living example?). Theo admitted many of his choices did include eating "humble pie."

On our podcast episode, Theo recounts a conversation he was having with his girlfriend at the time, who was a news reporter living her authentic dream:

> Well, I want to be a TV writer. She was like, well, what do you need to do to be a TV writer? I was like, well, I think I kind of need to move to Los Angeles. Okay, well then figure that out. It was very much point blank, it wasn't about us, whether she would make the move with me. It was about: what do you need to do to do the thing you want to do? And as soon as you define it, that does take a little bit of the fear out of it, because it's like,

you're calling it out, you know, you're putting it in existence.

(I want to repeat that this girlfriend of Theo's was living her dream at the time. In my opinion, it's a lot easier for someone to encourage someone else to do what's best for them from a position of also fulfilling their individual dream. She wasn't going with Theo.)

Imagine if you coached your kids, coming from a place where you are doing your thing. You are creating the art you want to create. You are entering those mixed martial arts championships you want to enter. You are experiencing real thrills because rather than settle for a shadow career, you are in the thick of what you really want to do. My husband suggested that I launch a podcast after he had attempted to launch his own. My equipment was originally meant to be his. He was also an early adopter of podcasts and I tend to consider trends at least five years later than the crowd. When he did his first and only interview, he realized the skills he was missing just happened to be the ones I was born to use. I am the extroverted, inquisitive, and extemporaneous thinker in our relationship. I made the first move when I asked him to dance in 1997. My husband knows my history of doing brave and imaginative things. He suggested that challenge because he knew I had it in me. In my life, it has been my personal fans who helped me see what I didn't see in myself. They knew me well enough to invite me to stretch myself because all of them believed that I wouldn't break. Let's imagine that you took what Theo's mom did for him and paired that with what his girlfriend said to him. Let's pair this combination and imagine what's possible for you in your busy mommy life.

I get that you are not a thirty-year-old childless guy right now. Theo's mom wasn't either. She was a single Black mom who taught music and played in jazz clubs. Don't settle for being in the shadow of moms who are challenging themselves and exploring their interests. Don't make up reasons why other people get to pursue their dreams and you cannot. You need all the energy you can get; comparing yourself to others to uncover why you wouldn't be able to succeed is an avoidable energy leak. For a mom who has to muster energy as it is, this can seem as deadly as a gas leak. Instead, it's essential to have your own personal fan; someone who sees and helps pull out in you what you are capable of. Someone to remind you to believe in yourself when you're struggling along a bumpy, dream-chasing ride. Don't feel shame either, for wanting to do something for yourself. Have you ever hidden the fact you are working on something for yourself? You didn't want your husband to catch you because, in your brain, you should have been doing the laundry or something for the household? I have, and it sucks!

Imagine what it would be like to have help to achieve your goals, instead of thinking you must do everything yourself. A lot of moms I've coached felt this way and it was not working for them; it's not going to stretch anyone's imagination. Let me introduce you next to a dad who has decided to impact "a billion people," in his words, not because he has extra time but because he knows how to network and enlist others in his mission. He is visible, consistent, and connected to his purpose. You may feel like you do not have anything in common with someone in the media, however here is where I want to bridge the gap. You do not need to want what he has to benefit from his wisdom. Trust yourself to let your imagination stretch as far as is right for you and your family. Wouldn't you want to see how someone who wants to impact more than a billion people thinks? I certainly wanted to. Let's see together.

Your turn to take what you've learned in this chapter to stretch your imagination. Use the following section to tailor the lessons you've uncovered from this chapter to fuel your imagination this week.

BIG IDEAS

- Treat your ambitions just like a professional would approach her craft
- Find your personal fan and enroll them in your dream
- Aim for the bull's eye of your dream not just somewhere in the proximity of it
- Eating humble pie, regardless of your credentials or wealth and setting your ego aside, is often the only cost of admission into your dreams

IMAGINATION WARM-UPS

1. Who are your personal fans? Use your imagination to think beyond your inner circle.

2. Out of that list, who might see your potential more than you can see it for yourself? Whose imagination can you count on? Enlist their help here.

3. Is there a path for you even if you are going into a creative world? What is it? Who is on it? How did they get good at their craft?

4. What can you hold onto so that your imagination doesn't go down a negative spiral and doubt doesn't set in, taking you into a shadow career rather than what you really want?

5. What sacrifices might you need to make? What flavor might your humble pie come in? How can you remind yourself that being happy is a worthy endeavor?

Chapter 20

BE UNAFRAID TO CHANGE YOUR MIND AND ASK FOR HELP
-DAVID MELTZER, AN ENTREPRENEUR AND PHILANTHROPIST

In this chapter you will:

- See that changing your mind is okay
- Understand networking is a choice and available to all
- Ask someone for help and uncover ways to help them as well
- Gain clarity in your purpose to be more confident before asking anyone for help
- Realize your imagination will help find the path forward

WHAT I WANT OUT of life has changed through the years. If you asked me what I wanted when I was a teenager, I would have said that I wanted to be a single, childless woman forever and have an amazing apartment in a global-city skyscraper. In August of my freshman year at NYU I wanted to bury my head in books and repel any guy who wanted to date me. I remember proclaiming in an NYU cafeteria to my two friends that I was done with guys. Two rejections in my eighteen years felt like enough. Two weeks later, at our first school dance, I found myself pursuing an upperclassman—he's now my husband. I guess the third time was a charm. It just goes to show that what we want *can* change.

As moms we are often the anchors of our families. We want to settle and build one home forever and never change. Many moms in my life have done just that. However, it's not written in stone and it may not feel right for you. So forget about what you said to your mom friends that you wanted to do this year; check back in with yourself. Does what you thought you wanted to do still feel right today? What if you could turn around and run in the opposite direction? Open yourself up to the possibility that things may have changed. It's okay to change your mind, maybe that's why we were given an imagination. Your imagination is there for when you do change your mind. If you trust it, and are honest about what you want, your imagination will know where to take you next.

My abuela told my mom I needed consistency and a solid foundation, which was true. However, I have not taken that to mean my feet need to be planted in one place and my home stuck in a time warp like my abuela did. I could close my eyes when I entered my grandmother's duplex in Miami and confidently navigate every room. Today, I could still tell you where all the bonbon bowls were located and precisely how her "Florida room" was furnished. Nothing changed in her house. Ever. So although I believe in giving my kids some consistency, showing them it's okay to sometimes change your mind is important too.

Your imagination can serve others as well as yourself, you can use it to lift up everyone. In your journey to use your imagination to change your mind, you will need to ask for help. You can use logical reasoning and a line of questions to pick the right people to mentor you on your journey. Former lawyers such as my podcast guest David Meltzer seem to be quite good at setting out rational arguments. David is the cofounder of Sports 1 Marketing and was formerly the CEO of the renowned Leigh Steinberg Sports & Entertainment agency (which inspired the movie *Jerry Maguire*). He helps his business-coaching clients "make a lot of money, help a lot of people, and have a lot of fun."

The first step David shared was that before we can work out whom to ask for help we need to identify what we want.

David says,

> I have five daily practices that I call the what,
> the who, the how, the now, and the why strategy.
> And as you know, the first thing that most people
> don't do is figure out their what, especially in your
> business, you probably have this all the time. So
> I take inventory of my "what" every day. I ask
> myself, What do I want personally, what do I want
> experientially? What do I want giving-wise to
> produce? And what do I want receiving-wise?...I
> also am not afraid—I also am not afraid of being
> a hypocrite. I'm not afraid of changing my mind.
> I'm not afraid of saying that I've grown and I've
> utilized the pain and mistakes of the past as an
> indicator, a turn signal, not a stop sign in my life.

Sometimes we stick to an idea or plan because we are
scared of what other people will think of us. Will they
think I was foolish? What if they think I made a mistake?
If I make a 180-degree change, will I feel embarrassed?
These questions are a key distinction I've noticed between
the most accomplished people and those who stay stuck
in a rut. The successful people I've interviewed, like
David Meltzer, treat life more like an Einstein Lab than a
Smithsonian Museum. They are more invigorated by the

number of experiments they can do in a day than by the number of achievements or possessions they can showcase for others to see. It's as if they get a kick out of getting back up after getting knocked down. No problem. Let me get in this other boxing ring. And other ring. Etc.

So now that you have this information of knowing what you desire doing and receiving, what's next? David says,

> The easiest way to get to where I want to be is to find someone that's already there and ask them for directions. And it takes radical humility.

So many moms that I've coached do not want to ask for help—for themselves. When it comes to their kids they may wake up an entire village with a yell, but for themselves... they wouldn't dare draw attention to themselves. What if we called on the same village to help ourselves? The village that helps us raise our children might also be open and able to lend us a hand as it relates to our personal ambitions. I think this is why radical humility is in order, especially for moms. How can we let ourselves off the hook for not looking out for ourselves? We aren't burdening others with our problems nor admitting we are weak. **In my experience a mom who seeks help is just as capable as one who shies**

away from seeking help. Once you can see that you are worthy of being helped your imagination will be stretched. Your imagination will stretch because when you ask for help, you will also want to uncover ways to help others. This is something David shared during our interview. So how would you exactly go about doing that?

This is what David has to say about mutual support:

> We have to understand that elevating others, first of all, elevates ourselves and that the way that we wish well on others is to be more interested than interesting. Find out what they're doing and find out what they like about what they're doing. Also find out what they don't like about what they're doing, then utilize a series of questions to see how our superpowers can help them with their weaknesses. We can also apply what we learn to another important aspect of the relationship, which is to find out how they can help us or who they know that could help us. And that approach alone, I think, is truly how we will raise all boats on that tide by being of service and value and asking for help.

What David is suggesting is ultimately networking. It's intentional. It's bilateral. What a lot of my clients who hate networking wrongfully assume is they won't have a lot to give. It's like the only outcome is that others are helping you. This is untrue.

Think about someone who is doing what you want to do. Maybe it's someone who is nailing motherhood, a mom who somehow manages to garden, make fresh meals, and makes her own vegetable-dyed tote bags, which she sells on the side. I know such a mom and her creative and bohemian lifestyle is inspiring. How does she do it? Especially as a homeschooling mom of five kids! If you wish you could live her kind of artsy and green life, then go ahead and ask her how she does it.

One day I was hosting a networking group for moms and I facilitated just such a conversation between a mom from California who lived in a concrete jungle and a Texan who lives an artsy and green life like the one I mentioned above. The Californian mom was so inspired by the Texan. In that moment, I decided to interview them both and what came out of that conversation was ways they could help each other. The Texan explained why she tossed her conventional thinking for more rooted family living. The Californian mom was motivated by the Texan's story. I was the spark who facilitated this mentor-mentee conversation. In that moment, I saw the opportunity. I hope by reading this book, you can consider this your spark to do the same in your life.

You may be thinking, who has time to go through this continuous loop of figuring out what you want, finding people who already have it, being of service to them, and then asking them for other people who might be able to help you? Many moms have told me that they didn't make time to network once they had children because it was hard enough to get work done, let alone stick around for after-work drinks. While this may feel like an impenetrable excuse, it really is a choice. You are entitled to make this choice. You get to decide if you want to bathe and read to your kids every night. You also get to opt out of work projects that were shoved on your desk because your boss knows you would never say no. It's normal not to network because it's outside of your comfort zone. Time is just the excuse many of us have decided to collectively use to avoid it.

In my conversations with working moms the real reason why they do not network is because they are uncomfortable doing so. You don't need to do after-work drinks, there are other ways. You can network over Zoom, on the phone, or with your fellow moms at a soccer field. Whatever works for you.

David says what is often the case isn't a lack of time but of confidence:

> I'm seeking the light, the love, and the lessons. I'm practicing ending fear, so that I'm not wasting time creating interference. I avoid [focusing on] shortcomings that create obstacles, such as the need to be right, the need to be offended, separate, inferior, superior, anxious, frustrated, angry, and guilty. Not only do they cause interference in your life, but they accelerate you in the wrong direction.

How do you feel about changing your mind and asking for help? What are your superpowers besides imagination? David is a great example of someone who needs the support of a lot of people to achieve his huge goal. He wants to touch over 1 billion people, hence his loop of constantly reviewing where he is and what he wants is important. So what do you want right now and whose help can you use to make the biggest impact humanly possible?

Asking for help often feels scary when it's just for ourselves. What if we can take our natural tendency to want to do more for others than ourselves and use it to stretch our imagination? So often charging for our services trips up moms yet this takes us out of many important conversations and it prohibits us from contributing financially to causes we care about. In the next chapter, you will explore how Japanese Zen money expert and millionaire Ken Honda sees money as a tool. He will help you think about the way you relate to money especially if you've ever felt as if you didn't have enough or could use more of it. What if something you do that comes out of your imagination could fund someone else's dreams? Money is important, and that's next.

Your turn to take what you've learned in this chapter to stretch your imagination. Use the following section to tailor the lessons you've uncovered from this chapter to fuel your imagination this week.

BIG IDEAS

- Get clear on what you want then ask yourself why, where, and how questions
- It's okay to change your mind, so don't beat yourself up when you want to or do
- Make networking a habit and have it play on a continuous loop
- Seek the light, the love, and the lessons rather than the reasons why something is not working or happening for you

IMAGINATION WARM-UPS

1. Imagine some of the big decisions you've made lately. Is there one that no longer serves you? It may be mom-related. Maybe delegate the laundry instead of doing it yourself?

2. What are two or three lessons you can imagine being helpful as you head in a new direction?

3. Imagine two or three people who are already where you wish to be. What questions would you ask them?

4. Where does your imagination go when you consider the things they may need your help with?

5. How can you creatively add networking into your daily life? What ways can you incorporate David's loop in your life?

Chapter 21

RETHINK YOUR RELATIONSHIP WITH MONEY
-KEN HONDA, THE AUTHOR OF _HAPPY MONEY_

In this chapter you will:

- Think about your relationship to money
- Explore an effective way to calm any stresses about money
- See the benefit of using the interests or skills that thrill you
- Gain a fresh perspective on why some people attract more money and why we need to revisit Altucher's energy framework
- Witness how being generous with your money can help you find the safety net for when the economy takes its dips

WHILE LIVING IN SYDNEY, Australia, I was surrounded by so many toned and youthful blondes. The weather was warmer year-round than where I came from; brrrr, Connecticut. It was the year I turned forty and I wanted to dedicate myself to my physical well-being. I knew myself enough to know I would be more committed to working out if I paid for a gym membership rather than relying on self-discipline. I also wanted better results. Could I get a six-pack after giving birth to identical twins who gifted me with some extra skin? I did not immediately join a gym, because I wanted to earn the cost of my membership. I felt that I needed to land a client to self-fund this experience.

As a little girl, I was taught a great deal about how to spend my money. Short answer: don't. My grandmother had lived through the Great Depression, so she was very frugal with her money, but my mom had the completely opposite approach. Typical of some people with manic depression, she would overspend during manic states. One day as a teenager I had to find, count, and put into a plastic resealable sandwich bag 120 pennies to take my two buses to school because there was no money at home. Imagine, as a teenager, the embarrassing sound of 120 pennies clanging one by one into a bus ticket machine. So the money choices you make today are very likely the result of complicated past experiences with money.

Thankfully, I signed a client so I joined the gym and I got my six-pack. So many of us have funny rules about money or investing in ourselves. Think about your relationship with money and how it relates to your mom script. A lot of moms I've spoken to would rather save their loot for kid activities or kitchen remodels than to take courses to learn something new or launch a business. But you can reimagine how you feel about, pursue, and engage with money. How your mom navigated money may be vastly different from how you do or want to. Does this ring true for you?

Let's explore money beliefs in this chapter because while you are off achieving your dreams, chances are you'll need to fund them and some of your dreams may become revenue generators that help you use money in angelic ways. I want you to think about not just making money but how you could use it.

Meet Japan's best-selling Zen millionaire Ken Honda. He was a really fun and extra-generous guest. His latest book is called *Happy Money: The Japanese Art of Making Peace with Your Money*, and it has sold 8 million copies worldwide.

During our interview Ken had this to say about money:

Money can become a weapon; money can be a healing angel. Money can become what you wish it to be. Money is just energy. Energy flows. So that's why some bad people are good at attracting money, because they become a very strong magnet. So whatever you do, if you have energy, money will be attracted to you. So this excitement energy is a source of this magnetism. So if you hate your job, you can't attract money, because you don't have that energy. If you want to attract more money, you have to be more attractive. This has nothing to do with your appearance.

You already heard from James Altucher how to create energy and the energy leaks to watch out for. Although Ken is not a mother, he is a parent and was his daughter's full-time caregiver when she was born, so he gets mom life. He says this about the reality of caring for a child and stepping away from a career or profession:

After about two years, I was lost, and I had also lost my way back. I couldn't find my way back to being an accountant, accountancy, and being a consultant. It's so far away, you know, where is the road? I'm lost. I know it's up there, but it's so high and I don't know even how to get back; I don't have the energy. After doing a lot of taking care of babies you get sleepy at 8:30 p.m. You know, especially if you have one more [child], that will take a lot of sleep away. So you can barely function as a human being let alone think of your career. That seems impossible, right? Maybe next life, so I know the feeling.

Several moms who decided to stop, pause, or downshift their careers (e.g., reduce their working hours or demote themselves) once their priorities got reshuffled agree that they too had no idea where to begin to generate the income they once commanded. If you've been out of the work scene then you might be able to relate to feeling like a fish out of water among high-flying working moms. It's intimidating to think if you go back, you might not be able to deliver; what if you are needed on the home front? Apart from wanting to see your kid during the school day, many moms I've spoken to would rather give away their commercial talents as volunteers than to be on the hook with a boss or a client. Same skills. Of course, this assumption that a mom can afford to give her time for free is wrapped up in some mom scripts. Try this: see if a dad feels the same way about using his skills in exchange for zero compensation. Exactly, they generally don't. Imagine a world where moms, instead of thinking volunteering was the only option, were paid to do what they enjoyed and were really good at doing? Oh, and they felt energized too? **Money can fuel positive change. Positive financial contributions will fuel you.**

Ken offers some guidance if you don't know what skill to commercialize.

> Imagine what excites you enough to stay up late? Do you have music to compose? Do you have a book to write? Do you have some kind of project that you also want to do before you die? What ideas are the ones that give you energy? Physically, I was exhausted at like 8 p.m. But I got so energized about my book ideas. So I had the energy to write my book, it was almost like a second rocket engine, right?

Some of the best revenue-generating projects have been launched by parents in between feedings or, heck, even during those feedings. You know you have the potential to be THAT badass, so don't ignore those moments.

It might sound Herculean, but Ken has this to say about how to get out of that initial step back into the world of commerce:

> You have to find five minutes, even when your kids are asleep or when they are in kindergarten or nursery care. You just find those precious five minutes or even three minutes in the bathroom.

> Try to come up with more creative ways so you can shine more. You know? You can start from the bottom of the occupation in this hierarchy of the society. You may start with laboring work or minimum-wage jobs, but you can move up by exchanging your gifts for money.

As I have always felt, since becoming a mom, when you are a parent your relationship to your time changes. Do you feel time spent on yourself is more precious than before becoming a mom? I'm not saying that you have less discretionary time than when you weren't a mom because that's obvious. Instead, what I mean is that one hour has to command a premium because it's an hour away from your kid(s). Well, this is why I want you to heed Ken's advice about how to uncover your purpose and ensure that money follows you. In my experience, I have gotten a lot of energy from charging for my coaching and it has helped me use money as an angel. I want the same possibility for you.

When my aunt was in her sixties, she had to move from her private apartment due to her financial situation. She was cash-strapped and ended up in an apartment-share situation with a stranger who should have been in jail. Things got unsafe for her, a woman who had always relied on herself for survival. Who wants to deal with moves and instability in their sixties? By this time I had figured out how to commercialize my skills and bravely ask for money in exchange, so I was able to give her a rental deposit for a studio apartment where she has now lived for years. I was able to use my money exactly as Ken suggests, as an angel. I didn't expect it to be repaid, though she did repay it, by showering my sons with gifts. If I hadn't worked out a way to use my skills to make money and had the courage to ask for it, I couldn't have helped my aunt gain her footing.

Here's how you can uncover the skill that can command the highest premium for you eventually so that you can be of the highest service to others too, in Ken's words.

> Let's say there are two florists. One who loves the flowers, and enjoys every second of her time being in the shop, and the other doesn't care about the job, he can be something else, he can be a baker, but he happens to be working as this florist. Where would you like to go? Where is more fun? Where is more fun energy flowing? In the first person's store, because she makes sure that the flowers are taken care of so well. In the other store, he doesn't even care to water the plants. So if you pour love, if you pour energy, to the things that you love, people will notice you.

That's how money energy will pay attention to you and come to you.

Think beyond just what you are really good at. You need to feel great using that skill too. There are plenty of people who can technically perform the same skills. Your enthusiasm is what will distinguish you.

Who wouldn't prefer to buy from someone who is extra excited about their industry, product, or services? Just think about your last pleasurable shopping experience. What made it fun? Would you have paid extra or used your word of mouth to share it with others? Did you feel the energy Ken mentions? You very likely enjoyed buying from that person and didn't feel icky at all about paying for that service. You may have even given the store clerk a tip!

Once you uncover the skills that you'd love to use then you too will be a magnet and the opportunity to ask for money will be there. My wish is that you seize the opportunity if not for yourself then to be of greater service to those you love. Ken offers us a warning that is evergreen in my experience because markets are cyclical. We don't need anyone to declare a global recession to incorporate this advice. Commercialize your top gift and then be open to generosity.

As Ken asserts:

> Generosity really pays off. Being generous and
> being kind to others is often discounted in
> society, unfortunately. But I think people will
> appreciate it more, because of the financial crisis
> we're going to experience in the next few months.
> I've been saying this for the past year, we're
> going to probably experience something big in
> the fall.

In Ken's case, he feels secure in his financial life for many
reasons, but one is that he can rely on the generosity of his
friends. Although culturally the U.S. and Japan are kilo-
meters apart when it comes to being financially transparent,
what you can learn here is that while money might be the
source of anxiety and stress, there is another way to play
your cards. It's important to know that while generosity is a
one-way gift it's also something that will come back to you.
Imagine the anxiety and stress you could free yourself of today, if you knew that because you've helped people financially they too would reciprocate, perhaps in other ways?
Ken said it: generosity pays off.

In my case, my aunt has been the stable emotional
support that I've needed during the tough times of my life
when others couldn't relate to my mom's mental health

challenges and choices. While being generous is not always about money, it's how the world works today and being of service in this way is tangible and useful whether you are the breadwinner or not. What if there was another way for you to contribute that you could do without any up-front costs? Could you imagine a way beyond participating in the world of commerce to add value to the lives of others? What if your most valuable resource is hidden in your life experiences? Let's dig in and stretch your thinking because while so many moms I've coached do not think their stories are that interesting, I've benefited from them and passed some along to you too in this book. You might want to recollect which stories stuck with you? Aren't you glad those brave souls decided to tell their stories? In the next chapter, you will see that your wisdom and the ideas inside your head might be truly valuable if you tell the right people. Let's go read how this can play out, and how to think about those times when your story or idea didn't align with the people you shared it with. Shall we?

Your turn to take what you've learned in this chapter to stretch your imagination. Use the following section to tailor the lessons you've uncovered from this chapter to fuel your imagination this week.

BIG IDEAS

- It's not inherently wrong to charge money for skills you'd do for free
- You can be someone's money angel
- You play a role in what you receive from your support system or others
- Generosity helps relieve the anxiety of feeling unsupported

IMAGINATION WARM-UPS

1. What comes up for you when you imagine yourself making a lot of money?

2. Where did your money beliefs come from? Imagine one old childhood money moment.

3. Brainstorm two or three ways money has been your angel.

4. Who might you want to fund or help if you had an extra $1K today? Imagine people or causes.

5. Sara Blakely, the founder of Spanx, sold her company and gave her employees $10,000 and plane tickets to anywhere in the world. What would you have gifted your employees if you had made billions from your brainchild?

Chapter 22

ACKNOWLEDGE THE IMPORTANCE OF TELLING YOUR OWN STORY
-JEFF BOLLOW, A SCREENWRITER/TEDX SPEAKER

In this chapter you will:

- Gain a fresh perspective as to why an idea that stays in your head is useless

- Reframe rejection and see it as misalignment

- Seek out people you align with to help you make your idea a reality

- Believe that your story is interesting even if you can't imagine how exactly so yet

- Learn to tell your story until you find an alignment

DURING THE PANDEMIC, I pitched my services to hundreds of prospective clients. I was offering to help them learn how to market themselves for new full-time corporate jobs. But I wasn't getting anywhere. I found they were feeling beaten down, resentful about their last workplace experience, and not interested in doing the same thing again. It was like I was selling them a horror screenplay and they were not into that genre.

At the time, I was hosting 1.5-hour sales calls and was rejected more than 300 times. I wondered what was going on. Something was very misaligned (and how many rejections could I take?). **I started to give what I was seeing a name. I came up with a phrase—career trauma.** I saw working moms suffering the most from this kind of trauma too. I wasn't sure what to do about it.

But as it turns out the pandemic did me a favor. Not only did it force me to take a break to think about my business, but it also forced me to do something totally different, something that would help other moms. It created the spark for my new focus as an imagination coach helping moms with school-age kids creatively deliver on their impact-driven entrepreneurial goals. This transition started during the first lockdown in Sydney when I had to homeschool my sons. I created an entire curriculum, using my imagination for my boys. I taught them about the moon, Mars, and Spanish, and I taught them how to clean up. (Do you like how I made a chore its own school subject?)

My fertile imagination was on display during these at-home school days. I drew on my childhood when I taught my Puerto Rican babysitter how to speak English. I had created a whole curriculum for her, complete with exams. This time, for my sons, I incorporated the world's best thinkers in my learning plan. I cherry-picked arts and crafts projects from the Berlin Museum Bauhaus, and we even took a deep dive into the mountains on Mars. Thanks, NASA, for those resources. My sons learned how to code using MIT's Scratch website. I thoroughly enjoyed making loads of things up. We tracked the moon phases for a month and every night I'd have my sons work on their penmanship, vocabulary, and astronomy all at once. We did this as a family, and at the end of the week each of them had to present their top learnings; out loud, for public speaking practice. I felt like the world was our oyster. My imagination was just getting fired up.

One evening I was looking for a TEDx talk about imagination, because I was beginning to realize it was an underutilized superpower. My search pulled up Jeff Bollow's 2015 TEDx Talk, "Expand Your Imagination Exponentially." Jeff was an American who had also lived in Australia like me. He has been a film industry professional for over thirty-five years and worked in every facet of the business.

Jeff believes that it's our job to show others what is in our imagination. Our story or an idea becomes valuable when we share it with others, or it won't make an impact on anyone. In Jeff's cinematic perspective, he says:

> So, for example, say I have a great idea for a movie, and everyone's going to love this idea. It's going to start a franchise and make a billion dollars. If I don't *do* anything with it, if all I ever do is *dream* about it—think about my scenes, the characters, whatever—but never sit down and actually write it, I can spend five years, ten years, twenty years thinking over and over about that idea. And I can make myself feel good about myself because I've come up with this world-changing story. But, in fact, it's never going to be a world-changing story because I'm not acting on it. All it's ever going to do is reinforce my own internal story, my own private narrative, what I'm telling myself. So I believe that our job, what we're here to do in this life, if you want to think in those terms, is to share our experience. To share our stories, to let other people see our imagination.

Ultimately, it's not about you. Your story or idea is not meant to stay in your brain. As Jeff says:

The thing is, as human beings, so much of what we perceive is subjective. Our brains, our imagination, the way we think—we're piecing the world together in our minds, making sense of it, through our ideas. An idea is not meant to be something that sits in your brain. An idea is meant to lead you to the next idea or action. So if you have an idea that you've been obsessing about for a long time, or you have an idea that you want to hold on to and protect and not let go, that's not good for you. It's obstructing your creativity. You need to take that idea, get it out of your head, and use it to get to the next idea. Every idea is designed to lead to either an action or a new idea.

If you want to have a profound impact you need to get in front of the people who will benefit from your story. It's important they are the right people; so how do you identify those people? Sometimes it is just by telling your personal story during a casual conversation or finding the right platform to tell your story. Jeff shared a great deal about being a producer who gets to pick screenplays that align with his interests and needs. Even if you have the script for the best horror film there is no point giving it to Jeff; he isn't into horror films, so you will quickly get rejected. In Jeff's words you will be misaligned; he swaps "rejected" with not being aligned.

Here's how he expressed this:

> We are aligned with different people in our lives. So when someone rejects you, it's not a rejection as such. It's just a lack of alignment. You're not aligned with that person, what they want, what they need, what they think is quality. I don't want to make horror films. When I was a young aspiring filmmaker, I saw that horror films were the easiest way to get in, because there's a huge audience for them. People love horror films. So I started imagining horror film ideas. I came up with absolutely horrific mental imagery in my mind. And I thought, I don't want to put this out into the world. Even if it made me famous, built my career, established me. I don't want to be responsible for those ideas existing in the world.

So, as I started feeling like I was casting my clients into horror movies, one zombie at a time, I realized I was in the throes of feeling misaligned. What I was trying to continue to do, what I had been very successful at in the past, no longer aligned with the people I was reaching out to. When I took a break and focused on using my imagination for the benefit of my kids, I started to see another way forward for me.

In January 2021, I attended a New Year's workshop with proceeds to benefit a nonprofit launched by a mom for children called Doodles Academy. I shared with the other people there how much fun it was to teach my sons during our lockdown and how I made it pretty epic. The founder of the nonprofit was inspired that I had figured out how to enjoy that time and bring in Montessori concepts to my home curriculum. I was flattered. This mom was involved in education and she thought I had something to teach her about teaching her child?

The combination of realizing I was no longer aligned with the clients I had chased and the fact that another mom had learned something from my story is why I committed to writing this book. It was a huge light bulb moment for me. Yes, my podcast is out there, but my instincts, the edits I have made to my mom script, and being open about my story should help more moms. I wanted to find my (new) people and realign myself.

I'm you.

I'm a mami who wants to be great, now. My idea was to share my story here, to add my piece to someone else's puzzle. I am doing this so other moms can see how powerful their imagination can be.

So many moms have ideas locked up inside of them. Stories. Ideas. Perspectives. Hopes. Why is it important to let them out? Why must you let other people see what you imagine? As a mom to three boys, I don't expect my book to shape how they father anyone. I do see the value that one day they can read about my inner thoughts. Maybe they'll be gentler partners? Or perhaps my journey will inspire them to stretch their thinking about whatever boxes people put them in? You have an imagination. You are learning how to use it. It's time to let your ideas out and tell your story. Telling your story will have the double effect of putting your ideas out in the world and help you find the right, aligned people who can help you make your ideas a reality.

How can you get in the mood to think creatively about the story you want to tell others? Jeff says: Play with your child. **Your child can be the missing piece in your puzzle.** Jeff mentioned how important playing is for us. If you read through the exercises that Chris Thomas Hayes shared, then you might already have played with your child. Here's a hint: do it again.

Jeff left us with these thoughts:

> As we grow up and as we mature, that play, that imagination, that sort of fantasy that we immerse into, can be used to extraordinary effect. So I think we need to celebrate it in kids. I think we need to celebrate it in adults as well.

Give these questions some thought after you play with your kid(s). Then decide that your story is important enough to be told. You've stretched your imagination to know that your story can help someone else. Now what if we can go back to that little girl you have deep inside? You know, the one who enjoyed her imagination and may have been the one to give you the idea that someday you'd live a glamorous life or become someone important? You will be inspired by an Olympian who managed to earn a gold medal despite the odds for a little girl who grew up in an impoverished home without money sometimes to get the food she needed to ready her body for Olympic success. If you have a dream locked inside that you thought of as a little girl then let this dream resurface. In the next chapter, you will know how to make that little girl proud and how she can help you really stretch your imagination and goals.

Your turn to take what you've learned in this chapter to stretch your imagination. Use the following section to tailor the lessons you've uncovered from this chapter to fuel your imagination this week.

BIG IDEAS

- You may be the missing piece in a bigger puzzle
- Your ideas need to get out of your brain to have any chance of an impact
- Sharing your stories inspires other moms to play bigger too
- A relatable moment or thought is a fertile seed for an interesting story

IMAGINATION WARM-UPS

1. Do you have a story you would like to share? Write down something you have done, or describe a solution that you think others can learn from.

2. What ways can you imagine telling that story or conveying your message?

3. Who are the people that would benefit from your story?

4. How can you connect with them?

5. Imagine the challenges that exist today. Which ones would you imagine feeling good about solving?

Chapter 23

MAKE YOUR INNER CHILD PROUD
-BREEJA LARSON, A GOLD MEDALIST

In this chapter you will:

- Be reminded of the enthusiasm and dreams you had as a child

- Wonder whether you may have made an impact on someone without realizing it

- Explore how you can use stress, pressure, or anxiety as powerful tools

- Use your inner child as your inspiration

- See the impact kindness can have on others

WHAT WERE YOU LIKE as a little girl? Sometimes even I forget how silly and comfortable in my own skin I once was. Many of our parents recycle stories about when we were young. My mom will tell anyone who'll listen about the time I was two years old attending a swimming lesson. My older peers were gripping onto the edge of the pool for dear life before class got started. Yet I was dog-paddling in the middle of the pool with a huge smile on my face. All I had was an archaic back float. As a child, I adored the water and was fearless. My mom was anxiously watching me from a window outside of the pool area. She was pretty proud and a bit nervous for me.

What about you? Were you a little girl who felt comfortable in her body and calm enough to do her own thing? Reacquaint yourself with that ball of energy, imagination, and optimism to harness your imagination. Remember the greatest parts of your younger self. This brings me to Breeja Larson, a gold medalist swimmer who competed in the London Olympics in 2012. She has a lot to teach us about leveraging our inner little girl to remind us about why we want to be great.

Breeja was originally born in Mesa, Arizona, one of seven girls. She grew up humbly and decided to do everything in her power to get to the Olympics. Originally inspired by a gymnast on TV, she eventually found her lane in swimming. When this podcast interview took place, she was hoping to qualify for the 2021 Tokyo Summer Olympics.

Don't worry. You don't have to aim for the Olympics to feel accomplished and fulfilled. I'm not here trying to stretch your imagination today by setting your sights on a gold medal. Unless you want one?

The reality is that Breeja shared many examples of greatness during my interview. Before we move into the ways you can stretch your imagination, I want to offer one deadly simple idea to be great this week. Breeja mentioned how moms (moms, just like you and me) shared their leftovers with her when she was a poor college student. Not just a typical poor college student but literally a student who couldn't afford a $6 jar of peanut butter because she was funding her own college experience. Imagine that: sending your kids leftovers for their friends to eat and those friends appreciating your generosity because otherwise they would have not eaten that day. And now to a different kind of greatness to really stretch your imagination...

At the age of four, Breeja was watching the 1996 Olympics and she was captivated by the gymnasts. In her words:

> I would do cartwheels in the front yard every day, until I was twelve years old and six feet tall and realized that it probably took more than cartwheels in the front yard to be an Olympian. I continued to do any sport that came my way

and tried to be the best at it and just kind of grew that competitive edge. In my senior year of high school, I found a local swim club. I started swimming but I wasn't paying my dues because I couldn't afford them. When the swim school kind of pulled me aside and sat me down to speak with me about it, I remember crying and telling them I was financially independent, and I couldn't afford it. I really wanted to go to college and an athletic scholarship was my best bet of paying for it. They allowed me to stay if I volunteered with the children and worked at some competitions. So I took it and I continued to work hard.

Perhaps you can relate? Personally, I was that little girl in elementary school, who was picked last for every team sport in gym class. The idea that I could excel in a physical endeavor was completely foreign. I didn't watch the Olympics growing up. I was more into *Columbo* and investigative dramas, which my mom always had on the TV in our apartment. Maybe that's where I got my interest in asking people all sorts of questions. **The point is that we each have an innate interest or strength from when we were little girls. Some of us have forgotten what they are.** I wonder, if we had stayed the course with them would we have achieved gold medals?

So let's say you want to stretch out your imagination. This is how. Ask yourself: what do I need to achieve the dreams I had as a little girl? Is there any way that I could build up the resilience I need? What about my motivation? What if I place the odds in my favor? Your imagination will level up, especially if you explore the innate interest or desire you had when you were a little girl. You need to uncover your ability to do anything you set your mind to. Breeja alludes to this. In her experience, it can be a question of having confidence and motivation.

Breeja thinks you can strengthen both and this is exactly how:

> Let's say confidence and motivation is a mental muscle. If you go to the gym in your mind, and consistently work on that confidence, it will slowly start getting stronger. It's just so slow and gradual that eventually you might look back one day and say, Wow, I am much more confident than two years ago. But if you stop working on it, those muscles are going to weaken, and then they're not going to be as strong. I don't think there's a magic number for how many repetitions it takes to strengthen a muscle whether mental or physical, it's about consistency. You need to go to the gym

consistently for the body type you're striving for, just as you need to go to that special place in your head mentally to strengthen your mental muscles. Some may only need to work on their mental muscles once or twice a day, others may need to constantly check in on their inner thoughts and chatter. Because just like the gym, we all need different exercises for different times, to look a certain way; it's the same with your mind. We all need to find which mental muscles we need to strengthen.

Life may be complicated for you at the moment, you may be caring for both your kids and your parents. I want to help you find a way to be great even in the midst of all that. Consider the following scenario.

Let's say you want to retrain as a teacher. You'll need to pass exams. You will feel pressure; it's better to embrace it as part of the journey. Find mindfulness tools that will help you instead of resisting the pressure. Earning a master's degree could be a requirement. Creating a portfolio will be important and a perfect use of your imagination. How do you plan to manage an unruly classroom? It's going to happen, so prep for it when you are calm. Time in the classroom will count. Prioritize getting this degree completed by using the times in your day, even tiny increments. A lot of things must get done to achieve your goal. Perhaps, as a little girl, you played teacher and your siblings were your students. Well, what if today you are in that sandwich generation? You are a caretaker for your aging parents and your young kids. How can you stay motivated to pass all those hurdles? What if you face setbacks along the way? Can you imagine picking yourself up or maybe pushing out your timeline to make the added pressure more manageable? As a child, with a mom with manic depression, I was told to avoid pressure because it could break me. My mom often experiences psychotic episodes in stressful situations. However, I've been known to embrace pressure like Breeja; perhaps you should too.

This is what Breeja says about pressure:

> I think pressure is a tool. I think the reason why we don't appreciate the pressure is because it's scary. We don't want to be brave and take it on. If you're someone who tends to worry a lot, or has high anxiety, learning how to manage pressure is very powerful too. You just have to learn how to handle it, instead of it handling you. Because it's scary. It's uncomfortable; no one likes to be uncomfortable. But if you can thrive and learn to be comfortable with the uncomfortable, just

imagine how much better everything would be. So learn how to use your worrying or your stress or anxiety as a tool and realize that it helps you get things done. Keep striving forward and use that pressure to keep performing the way you want to. Then I feel your performance and your productivity can rise to a whole new level.

You are not supposed to break. This is not about compromising your sanity or health. You have an opportunity to get creative about how you perceive pressure. What if you are under a lot of pressure caring for your parents and kids? Right now, you know becoming a teacher is who you were meant to be and what you were meant to do. You have a compelling reason for it. You must take action and learn how to be brave. Stretch your imagination so that you can figure out how to handle it for yourself. As a mom, you may have noticed that life continues even if you feel crappy or worn out. The days pass by, even if you witness them or they fly away. This is why you need to be great now. Your sense of urgency can't just be used for everybody else. You've got to turn it on yourself too. There are some ways you can experiment with to see what will help you stay motivated and gung ho about your goal. Stretch your imagination by asking yourself: how can I use pressure as a tool in my life? You will want to know what having a stretched out imagination looks like in your life. Go back to when your imagination was totally awake, down to play anytime, and ultra-bendy. Breeja found a way to engage with her inner child. Imagine yourself back when you were role-playing being a teacher to your siblings or that first time you thought up your goal as a child.

This method helped Breeja; here's what she had to say about this:

> One mental trick that I'll use a lot of the time, if I am in a situation where I'm lacking motivation, and I just don't want to be there: I'll think, what would ten-year-old Breeja say? Would she be proud? Would she see this image of what I'm doing now and look up to it? Would I be a role model for her? And having that really cuts a little deeper for me, because I just believe that there are so many children out there who deserve so much more. They have the potential and talent. I refuse to believe that the upper class holds the talent, though they may have the resources; talent is widespread.

Go back to yourself at that young age. Do this when you are tired or feeling unmotivated. How would your younger self want you to behave? Will you be staying up one hour later tonight to submit your paper? What vision of yourself can you keep close to your heart so that it can motivate you when you need it? What did you imagine being possible as a kid? What would you have been awestruck about in the person you are today? What questions would inspire you to take action when you feel the least motivated to do so? Answering this question is your shot at stretching your imagination as far as it can go without breaking. Test your imagination: imagine yourself at the age of ten or four. This worked for an Olympian. Your imagination can go back there because that is when it was at its height. Breeja, at four years old, was looking at gymnasts and thinking she could be like them too. This was all her doing in her heart. It was natural. This is not to say there will be days when you don't feel like working over-overtime. It's then that you can implement this other tool: a mood color chart. I love this tool so much that I have implemented it in my life and coach moms to do the same. You can take a deeper dive into your motivation levels too.

Breeja explains how a mood color chart has helped her:

> One of the things that I really enjoy doing is a color chart, I have a mood color chart that has all the months and days just on a single piece of paper. Depending on my mood that day, I will

color in that day with a corresponding color. If I start seeing a pattern where two months ago, I was really happy and the colors kind of shifted and now not so much. I'll ask myself: Why? And you know, it might simply just be because I'm hitting a sugar craving and not eating sugar and as a sugar addict, you know, this is affecting my mood. So is that it? Or when was the last time you talked to your parents or your siblings? Or you know, what books are you reading? What media are you listening to? That can have a big effect.

We all have cycles. The key is to understand our own. What gets you lackadaisical? If you've watched ads for KFC, then it's no wonder you ordered a bucket of chicken last night. Not everything is out of your control. Your elderly mom might wet the bed tonight. That is not in your control. However, whether you've fatigued your adrenals because you overdid it on caffeine you can do something about that.

It's important to have tools in advance that can help you stay your course. Your imagination will stretch again if you give it the clues it needs to know when to use its expanded capacity. All of this is intentional and can be preplanned because it's hard to keep an Olympic schedule, as hard as it would be to keep up your schedule if you wished to become great in any capacity.

I'm not going for the Olympics myself but Breeja's extraordinary understanding of what will get her into a cold pool, day in and day out, is what I urge you to uncover. We all have our own drivers. When things do not go as planned that is when we'll need to remind ourselves of our ambitions. You've noticed my intention is to show that seeking unmom-like ambitions is not a selfish goal. It's life-giving and a positive addition to your family's well-being. Without something fun or fulfilling going on for yourself, you are left to relying on the accomplishments of your kids to fill a void. Motherhood is not the end of your life. It's an opportunity for you to test, navigate, and fill in the gaps from your youth so that there can be progress across the generations. Otherwise, as families the risk is that we too are just a bunch of political parties vacillating between power and undoing what the prior generation did, and ultimately staying the same. Breeja's goalpost was foreign in her family. She had to push herself into the right circles. All of this takes a ton of foresight. Yet, what kept her going turned out to be her awareness for whom she was doing this...that little girl who originally thought being an Olympian would be a fun idea.

Your turn to take what you've learned in this chapter to stretch your imagination. Use the following section to tailor the lessons you've uncovered from this chapter to fuel your imagination this week.

BIG IDEAS

- Find the tools that work best for you under pressure or to motivate you
- Don't disappoint your inner little girl. In some cases, you'll literally be disappointing other little girls
- Believe that you want more because you have more inside
- Use pressure as a tool not a crutch
- Monitor your mood

IMAGINATION WARM-UPS

1. What did you feel drawn to as a little girl? What things stretched your imagination as a child?

2. Imagine all the tools you may need to achieve your dreams or to be great. Which ones feel fun or playful?

3. What sort of cues can you imagine being helpful over the course of the next two weeks?

4. What does your inner child look like? Is there a certain age in your life when you were super imaginative?

5. Imagine the last three days, what was your mood like? How might you imagine changing it?

LET'S BRING THIS BACK to moms like us. I'm so proud that you have explored ways to reawaken, play with, and stretch your ability to imagine what's possible for yourself. There might be things that you stumbled upon that feel so out of reach because some of my case studies included non-moms. I included insights and wisdom from an Olympian, screenwriter, and a *Sesame Street* puppeteer, because they had important lessons for us. As moms, we do think differently once we are in charge of someone else's well-being and quality of life. Our choices are personal at the DNA level. Whether you adopt a child, birth one, or take on the role of being a mom in any other way, you are now a mom. But that doesn't mean you can't learn something from someone who isn't a mom, you're not taking parenting lessons from them. My intention is to show you what using your imagination, a universal human quality, can do if used to its fullest capacity. You just may have to adapt their ideas to work for you.

So under those conditions of someone who cares d-e-e-p-l-y for her children, what then would be possible and worthwhile to split your life's dedication to? Is there anyone who has used her imagination in a way that is grounded by metrics? Impact or income? Regardless of how you intend to use your imagination, just take a look at what another mom has accomplished for the world. Consider the story of a mom who was raised by a single mother with a humble beginning who has achieved something totally breathtaking. Her impact and the financial contributions of people around the world might convince you that nothing is really off-limits—especially if you are a nurturing mom. You can even decide to use your imagination and its output to nurture the world. This sentence makes me want to do more right now...

Case Study

GO BEYOND WHAT YOU CAN IMAGINE AND LAUNCH A MOVEMENT
-ASHA CURRAN, THE CEO OF GIVINGTUESDAY

MY ABILITY TO SEE the greatness in other people, even when they can't see it in themselves, is homegrown. There are plenty of skills you learn as a result of having a mom with frequent manic-depressive episodes and a dad who teaches you how to shield yourself in an unforgiving world. This training taught me how to use my imagination to see the greatness in myself when it was only me and my mom. I also used it to find great people who could help me navigate a sea of not-so-great people.

My coaching clients are really great people. They are people who want to help others. One particular client, who had worked at an elementary school for years, knew she wasn't living up to her potential so she turned to me for guidance. Two weeks into our engagement she revealed a good deed that really touched my heart. She told me about a student at her school who was physically disabled and because this little girl didn't have a special-needs bike she couldn't ride to school with her friends. This moved my client to take action. She asked for donations to help this child, and as a result of her success in doing so that little girl got her own special-needs bike and was able to ride a bike just like her peers.

When was the last time you felt moved into action? Did you do something about it? Ask yourself: if not, what stopped you? It was really important to my client that she did everything in her power so this child had the same tools as others at her school. Yet, when it came to her own career, she could not find the same determination to act for herself. Why did she find a way to make mountains move for that little girl but was unable to create the same motivation and drive for her own benefit?

She didn't have to muster up the courage to pitch her own skills and talents to amass the donations. She felt like it was her moral obligation to act on behalf of this child. This is what propelled my client over the finish line. If it was just about her, then her courage would have failed her. There are many forces at play that stop us from stepping into our greatness. You can be in love with your list of dreams. However, if you have deep-seated insecurities, get ready to battle with impostor syndrome every step of the way.

You never know where a simple act of kindness or generosity will lead to, especially when an idea first pops into your head. Meet Asha Curran, the CEO of GivingTuesday. The GivingTuesday movement started as a hashtag and today it operates globally, utilizing the spirit of generosity that resides in each of us. One year the organization secured 1.3 billion USD in donations **in one day**. I invited Asha on my podcast after researching her on behalf of a coaching client who was interviewing for a nonprofit job. I saw that GivingTuesday was coming up and when I was mock interviewing my client for that interview, I encouraged her to imagine GivingTuesday ideas for the virtual interview. I always encourage clients to think outside of the box. This is my favorite part about coaching. They do not wait for permission for fresh ideas. I wanted this to knock the socks off her interviewers.

Asha has a humble backstory. She was raised by a single mother on the Lower East Side before the cool bars took over that part of NYC. Asha's journey began when she attended one of the private all-girl Seven Sisters Colleges—Mount Holyoke College in Massachusetts. This is where she saw women empower one another.

In Asha's words:

> What I loved so much about Mount Holyoke was that when you are in a community of just women there really is something different about how you speak to each other, how you support each other, and how open you are with each other. There's a special kind of fierceness that comes with being part of a community like this. I also saw the Women in Power Fellows [the women's fellowship program Asha also founded] offering each other that same kind of unconditional support and inspiration. That's very special, when you have it with a friend, right? But there's something about being told you can accomplish extraordinary things professionally. Right? That is very, very validating, and kind of shockingly rare, even for really extraordinary women. It's too rare.

Asha Curran is a great example of a working mom who was inspired into building and leading a global movement. Does the idea of mobilizing a team and volunteers around the globe to raise donations like Asha did intimidate you? My heart would skip a beat if I was on the hook for that number, even if I had a global dream team.

I had to know if Asha was like me. Did she feel fear?

> I think I'm probably only fierce as an antidote to
> my fear. If I let my impostor syndrome [win], my
> insecurity takes over, I could see that happening.
> And so I fight against it. The way that I fight against
> it is by being as fierce as I can. But it's not that I
> don't feel that inner turmoil or that inner anxiety.
> I think we all do. I read once that men and women
> feel impostor syndrome equally, but that women let
> it stop them and men don't.

Don't let fear stop you. There are many antidotes to fear.
You can act in spite of fear. You can seek out scary situations.
You can even fearfully get to the top of a bridge and back.
To overcome this feeling and embrace a challenge you don't
have to just rely on your own imagination. Asha Curran
allowed herself to grow with GivingTuesday. It wasn't only
her imagination.

> I just grew deeper and deeper into it every year
> and my dreams for what it could accomplish
> got more and more and more aspirational, not
> because my own mind expanded but because
> of my own vision and imagination. Because of
> what I saw happening. It was everybody that

was engaging with GivingTuesday that made me
believe in the hugeness of possibility.

She grew into this movement. I see a comparison to how we
grow as moms. Imagine if someone dropped a teenager on
your doorstep. Suddenly you must learn their preferences,
character flaws, and thinking patterns overnight. Over-
whelming thought, right? Thank goodness it doesn't usually
happen this way. Typically, after we give birth, we pick up
our parenting know-how as we grow and develop together.
We evolve and adjust as that baby eventually turns into a
teenager.

It is the same concept with a big goal. You don't
begin knowing how to do everything on day one. At the start
you are moved by something. You take one step forward.
Chances are it's a small one at first. The size of the step is not
the point. You are moving toward your goal. As you move in
the direction of your goal you may cause a reaction in others.
Someone might see you taking action. You might encounter
like-minded people. The reaction may just be internal. You
might just feel proud of yourself. You said you would write
a newsletter and here you are hitting Save on your 500-word
newsletter. Go, you!

Take enough steps and you will begin to feel
momentum. Do this enough and you won't be able to stop
yourself from talking about this goal. People will know about

your goal and may want to help. If nothing else, people will wonder what got into you. Why are you so happy? If you are moved, then it's highly likely other people will also be moved.

In the case of GivingTuesday, Asha has this to say about what drives movements:

> Your voice joined with all of these other voices saying similar things, wanting a similar thing. Dreaming about a common vision is really, really powerful. You're inspired to do more, to say more, to become more involved in whatever it is. That's certainly been my perspective with GivingTuesday. People do one small thing and then they say to us, this is amazing. I think I want to do more. I want to do other things. What else can I do?
>
> The people who love it the most become leaders within the movement, they become leaders at their organizations, they become leaders of countries, they become leaders of local communities. They think maybe I'm involved in this particular cause, maybe it's climate change, but I want to actually build a coalition, a whole community. People in organizations who care about this one thing, so I'm not just going to push forward by myself,

I'm going to actually link arms with a bunch of mission-aligned people and form a coalition. Then I think you start to really have a semblance of a movement because you have individuals, you have groups, you have organizations, you have coalitions, you have local communities, all who are pushing toward this common goal in their own way.

You can see how Asha's experience at college has influenced how she works. Working collaboratively has so much potential. If a large group of people share a vision, they will work productively together by supporting and encouraging each other. We may feel we need to do it all alone. If you feel moved by an injustice or see a possibility for a positive change in your world, then I promise you there will be other people who will feel moved too.

We are living a shared human experience. Interviewing hundreds of people and coaching hundreds more has taught me that we have more in common than not. This includes the things that give us goose bumps or bring up tears. You will find your crew. You and your crew will also crave to contribute more. We want to contribute. It can even be addictive.

Whatever your goal is, know you only need to do what you can. You will still get a reaction from doing something.

You will learn things. You'll build your confidence too. If you are moved by your goal then you'll want to do more. You will also want to be more to make a bigger impact. **You can grow into your big vision. Count on this.** Rather than think about how you don't know how to build a website or be a fundraiser, think about the skills, talents, relationships, and experiences that you do have. Then use your imagination to identify ways you can help the person or entity you would like to help. Use your imagination to come up with a fierce identity that you can embody before acting. Beyoncé embodies Sasha Fierce as her alter ago when we see her onstage. If it's good enough for Beyoncé, it's good enough for you—**fellow warrior mom**.

You heard Asha's story and you might be thinking to yourself, I'm not trying to bite off more than I can chew. It's normal and perhaps if Asha knew, when she agreed to lead this effort, how massive the impact of GivingTuesday would become, she wouldn't have signed up. The point is that it's time to honor yourself. Your opinions, decisions, relationships, skills, resources, compassion, and your imagination—honor all of it. If you want to make a global impact, start locally and see where things go from there. Whoever you most admire today was probably in your shoes once, filled with disbelief or self-doubt. The difference is that they decided to give their ambition a try. Cross a bridge. Nurse twins. Snag interviews with millionaires.

My adventures have been the moments when I decided to ignore my insecurities. I knew during those journeys that whatever I set down to start a challenge would rear its ugly head up. I just didn't let it block me at the entrance of a pretty fun theme park of a life moment or challenge. Angels popped up for me along the way, however it's safe to say that I was seeking them. With successful experiences behind me I was able to more quickly decide when to take on projects. It has also been with many failures behind me that I could see that I can handle more than my mom was able to because of her mental illness (not due to her character). It's a worthy activity to reread the mom scripts you've inherited. It's impossible that it was ever meant for all moms to play our role the same way. Modernity wouldn't have it like that. Today moms have different challenges than prior generations. But some problems are the same; they might only persist because we've forgotten to use our imagination. You have a part to play in the progress of humanity and it goes beyond being a mom to your children. It's entirely up to you to decide where to step in and whom to follow along the way. For me, it's you right now, as you are considering how to morph yourself into the kind of mom that you were truly meant to be.

Your turn to take what you've learned in this case study to go beyond what you can imagine being possible with your newly stretched imagination. Use the following section to tailor the lessons you've uncovered from this chapter to fuel your imagination this week.

BIG IDEAS

- You have enough to launch a movement. Want to?

- Celebrate other moms and women

- You will learn as you go and you will grow in the process

- Momentum can work in your favor and make magic possible

IMAGINATION WARM-UPS

1. Who are the people who will benefit from your efforts? Is there one person you can focus on whenever you are scared to act? Imagine them.

2. What steps can you take to get started on your goal?

3. Who else might be moved by this topic? Can you ask other like-minded people for ideas?

4. What can you do locally? Observe what's needed in your own community.

5. Did you uncover any skill gaps? If you could wave a magic wand and pick up some skills that you feel you are missing, what skills would those be? Bonus: YouTube is a great classroom. Use your imagination to fill your tool belt or to reach out to the YouTube content creators who know how to do a skill. Ask for their help.

CONCLUSION

I'M SUPER EXCITED you made it to the end. You should now have the awareness to be your strongest, most nimble, playful, and energized self. In this book, you uncovered how to regain your self-trust in baby steps, how to map future steps more confidently, and how to draw the power you exhibited when you decided to become a mom and reach higher than you've ever dreamed. You will have awoken, played with, and stretched your imagination, which should now be brimming with fertile ideas.

You may also be sitting there thinking, "Is Melissa crazy? I have the longest to-do list waiting for me. There's laundry. I am trying to manage the logistics of my daughters' music lessons. Tonight I will have to hide in my home office instead of eating dinner to read all the school emails. I have a ton to do in the next three hours. The thought of applying what worked for Beth, Ken, Suzy, Chris, or any of these people is giving me hives. What does Melissa want me to do with all this information?"

The pressures of being a mom are constantly evolving. Our families, communities, and clients or bosses will continue to have ever-changing needs. How can we keep our proverbial ax sharp to handle what the world hands us or what our hearts call on us to produce? How can we take our own needs and dreams into consideration? So isn't it better to ready yourself with the greatest superpower you have? Your ability to imagine anything?

At the beginning of this book, I mentioned my abuela, one of thirteen born on a farm in Cuba with an eighth-grade education. She planted the seed for me to become a professional. What if your fertile ideas inspire your future generations too? I believe the journal prompts in every chapter, will help you accomplish just that. Meanwhile, the free quiz on my website can point you in the right direction as to where to focus your efforts. Take the quiz to learn about your Imagination Wellness Assessment, which can help you understand why you may not be bringing your best yet as a mom and current (or aspiring) business owner. I would love to hear what popped up for you when you did this. Email me to let me know, you can find me at melissa@fertileideas.com. The journal prompts are just the beginning. Imagine if, as a collective of moms around the world, we all made the commitment to using motherhood as an opportunity to apply our imaginations to make a difference. Imagine if each of us decided to use our fertile imagination to come up with a compelling vision of what we would like to see more of in the world? One vision, millions of moms, one potent superpower? We have the tools we need to fuel and sustain this effort. I don't need to squint to see if I can imagine this powerful vision. It's clear that any mom with a fertile enough imagination can come up with her own way to create an impact and to make a pair of mom jeans work for herself.

What I've imagined is this: moms exploring and experiencing all that life has to offer them with the same sense of unfiltered joy we see in our kids. Let's make that vision real, shall we? Will you join me in making this a reality? It can all start with you. I can help you. Two fertile imaginations are better than one. Visit www.fertileideas .com to uncover the best coaching option for you that includes data-driven accountability, a focused game plan, and a playful spirit to pull you forward to the finish line of your next big idea. Do you not yet have your most fertile idea? This is why I created the **Imagination to Impact Five-Day Challenge**. This is the perfect starting point to help you focus on coming up with the one big idea that will set your life in the ultimate direction where your skills, interests, experiences, and relationships can facilitate your maximum impact. What makes this challenge unique and useful is that you will see what having a fertile imagination can look like with your kids in tow! Imagine getting to experience the full life you desire and knowing that your kids are reaping the daily rewards too? What if by uncovering your fertile idea you realize what lights up your child or brings a smile to their face? Or listen to my podcast *Unimaginable Wellness*. Your dream can be tailored to your lifestyle (remember Chad, the founder of Kick Ash Basket®?), even if you can't imagine pulling it off now with the kids in tow. We do have an example that has worked for a fellow mom, years ahead of us; ahem, remember Martha? Ultimately, I truly believe that both your dreams and those of your kids can be achieved side by side.

Let's get you there first and then together we can inspire the next generation of moms to use their superpower too. Sound like a plan?

www.fertileideas.com

If you enjoyed reading this, please leave a review on Amazon. I read every review and they help moms discover my books. What if your review starts a ripple effect to inspire a mom just like you to rediscover her imagination and set forth on her own quest to make a maximum impact? Will you help me spread the word?

INTRODUCING
UNIMAGINABLE WELLNESS
HOSTED BY MELISSA LLARENA

You are a mom in the thick of it with big entrepreneurial ambitions. You are running on all cylinders and do not want to slow down. You want to proactively navigate anxiety, overwhelm, depression, exhaustion, burnout, and diaper blowouts because you can't afford to compromise your wellness. Your wellness in every category of your life is essential to your success as both a leader and a mom. So here's the good news: motherhood came bearing gifts—you now have access to an explosive superpower that can help you avoid, navigate, and get through the ups and downs of entrepreneurship, motherhood, and life. You now have the explosive power of your fertile imagination, which is not only an unexpected competitive edge, birthed during motherhood, but also the key to helping you achieve unimaginable wellness so you can sustain a healthy pace and stay present when necessary for overall longer-term mom life success. Sound good? Start listening....

Join Melissa and her guests, including GaryVee, Suzy Batiz, Beth Comstock, James Altucher, Fran Hauser, Dr. Joel Fuhrman, Lisa Messenger, and Cal Fussman, on Tuesdays for new episodes focused on how others have stretched their imagination for maximum impact. You can count on Melissa to weigh in on how a mom can tailor this wisdom into even the most emotionally and mentally overstretched life. She gets it, as a mom to three high-energy boys and an entrepreneur since 2011. She carried her firstborn in an Ergobaby to her first sales pitch and two years later birthed identical twin sons. It's been one blowout after another, and in this podcast Melissa shares her lessons learned as well as interviews some of the most dynamic humans in the world who are operating at the fringes of their imagination so that you can optimize yours.

Scan this QR code

to subscribe now on

and wherever you listen to your favorite podcasts.

WHAT LISTENERS ARE SAYING

Powerful conversations

Melissa leads these powerful interviews with curiosity, not leaving one stone unturned. She is relatable and her guests have interesting experiences to share. In her own words, these experiences "will change something in you." I do believe so!

Inspiration & Motivation

An inspiring podcast for every woman who needs a little motivation and empowerment to get out there and live their best life! An opportunity to connect and relate to other moms following their dreams and making a difference.

Excellent and informative

In each, Melissa's comfortable way of interviewing elicits meaningful and practical insights. For anyone who is a mother, the wealth of information offered can serve as a guidepost and a companion to the journey we as parents are on.

ACKNOWLEDGMENTS

To my biggest personal fan my husband, Jesus: You've been committed to seeing me soar and reach my potential. This is something I could have never imagined on the day that the sun shined on you back at NYU, when I first took notice of your splendor. Thank you for the moments when you toggled between fatherhood and breadwinnerhood and for that time you stretched into a new role and joined me as a Pandemic Emergency Co-Teacher in 2020. You are **why** I was able to put together this book. I want to also acknowledge you for being someone who is able to see more in me than I have ever been able to see in myself, at least not since I was seventeen.

To my three sons, Gabriel, Nick, and Noah: Thank you for adding daily humor during my book-writing process by making it a point to find all the bad words in this book. You remind me every day to play more. You've been around for all of my entrepreneurial adventures. Gabriel you are my Chief Heart Officer. You joined me on that first sales meeting. Our hearts were pressed up against each other while riding the NYC subway to the infamous Le Pain Quotidien, where I launched my coaching practice. Noah you are my Chief Inquisitive Officer. You asked me why I host my podcast, and this was the day I changed its name and focus to align with whom I wanted to impact, moms. You helped me align my podcast with my identity. Nick you are my Chief Playing Officer. You have been in charge of theatrics and laughter during ordinary days. You've turned things around and helped me be present since your birth. Every night I give the three of you secrets, and here's one that's okay for the world to know that I have whispered into your ears: the world is huge and you get to create your own life experience. My wish for the three of you is that one day you bring your own fertile ideas into the world.

To my mom, Esther: My fertile imagination came in part from my early-life experience with you and it may even be genetic. Some research suggests that kids of those with manic depression tend to be artistic or creative. Thank you for this gift. The world is suffering with mental illness as are you, but being by your side stretched me to be tenacious and greatly fertilized my imagination. Your manic highs raised the roof on what I could do and the lows woke up my imagination. It's also important for you to know that you did get to play every role you once desired. You got to be a nurse, doctor, chef, working mom, and stay-at-home mom. You got to be everything you had ever imagined. The costume was the same. You wore your mom hat. The same can be said by the moms for whom I wrote this book, too. **Every** mom gets to play a ton of roles. Thank you.

To my dad, Joseph: I've been listening. You have taught me a heck of a ton of life skills. You taught me about being street smart, saving money, tenacity, persistence, chutzpah, and being unafraid to ask for help. You never ever put a cultural glass ceiling above me in terms of what I could accomplish. I would not (nor could not) have done half of the things that I mentioned in this book if you hadn't built me up in your own way. Recall back in the '80s, '90s, '00s, when you'd ask me to go into gas stations to ask for directions? Apparently, bravery in speaking to strangers is a transferable skill! Your inquisitive nature also rubbed off as did your creative and unconventional thinking about overcoming challenges. I want to acknowledge you for being the best dad a girl could have.

To my sisters, Lori and Reyna: Lori you are always enthusiastically encouraging me to keep doing incredible things and I hope this book serves as inspiration in how you decide to bring all of yourself to motherhood. Reyna, you are now a mom and you have already figured out that motherhood is a journey for which there is no perfectly laid out path. May you both always feel empowered to bring your own fertile ideas to life.

To my friends, who have been encouraging me for a lifetime in some cases including all my mom friends around the world and women who are not moms: You each play a special role in my life.

To my book editors, including Amanda McMahon: Thank you for helping me bring this book together and for saying, "it's your book," along the way. Your words helped me overcome several moments of self-doubt. Laura Carney, thank you, too.

To all my writing advisors, including those who helped me early in my writing-healing journey before becoming a mom: Christian Simamora, the late Mrs. Pender, and Ms. Cullens.

To all my beta readers and book launch team, including Macollvie J. Neel, Katherine Howell, Dr. Sylvia Gonzalez, M.D., Maureen Turner Carey, Alejandra Molina, Zennia Csikos, Kathryn Doherty Gale, Kimberly Smith, Ximena Sanz de Santamaría, Margaret Trietsch, and those who offered insights and cheerleading along the way.

To all my podcast guests, including everyone whose story has been included in *Fertile Imagination*.

To all of my clients over the last twelve years: Your stories will always be held in my heart. Let this encourage you to write your own story because you are worthy and interesting.

To all the libraries in the world, including Stanton Library in Sydney, Australia, where I began to write this book, and the Westbank Community Library in Austin, Texas, where I completed it.

To everyone who has touched my life! My intention is that this book touches your life back.

To the copywriter I left hanging years ago, I am finally turning in my assignment.

ABOUT THE AUTHOR

MELISSA LLARENA is on a mission to encourage, embolden, and empower one-million-plus entrepreneurial moms by teaching them to reawaken the power of their imagination and apply a more playful approach to navigating life's hurdles. She wants them to make a massive impact.

She is a coach, consultant, speaker, contributor to ForbesWomen articles that have garnered 4 million-plus views, and the host of *Unimaginable Wellness,* the podcast for entrepreneurs, founders, and creators who are moms. Featured guests include GaryVee, Suzy Batiz, Jordan Harbinger, and Beth Comstock.

An online entrepreneur since 2011, Melissa launched her business in parallel to becoming a mom the first time around. One set of identical twins later, Melissa brings a decade of experience working for Fortune 500 brands and over another decade as a solopreneur. She holds a psychology degree from New York University and an MBA from the Tuck School of Business at Dartmouth, and a Transformational Coaching Academy certificate based on Tony Robbins's principles and Landmark Education insights. She's becoming a meditation practitioner, enrolled in The Mindfulness Meditation Teacher Certification Program with Tara Brach and Jack Kornfield. Her perspective has also been influenced by having lived for three years in Sydney, Australia, as an ex-pat family, and prior to motherhood, she worked and lived in NYC, London, and Paris. You can read her story "Imagine A Better Way" (Woodhall Press, 2023) in the anthology *Fast Fallen Women*. Melissa currently lives in Austin, Texas. Visit www.fertileideas.com for resources and speaking opportunities. Follow her @melissallarena.

www.ingramcontent.com/pod-product-compliance
Lightning Source LLC
Chambersburg PA
CBHW030352130626
46549CB00004B/1457